# Commu

## A Look at Life on the Rails

Nygel Worthington

# Commutication: A Look at Life on the Rails

Published by Eric Bailey

e.3ailey@gmail.com

South Orange, NJ 07079

ISBN: 978-0-578-83113-8

Library of Congress: 1-7633589591

Registration Number: TXu002149403

Cover design by Eric Bailey

Thank you, God, for the idea.

The conversations documented in this book are real. First names, company names, middle names, surnames, mother's maiden names, nicknames, pet names and last names, personal addresses, business addresses, email addresses, little black dresses, home phone numbers, cellular phone numbers, fax numbers, office numbers, social security numbers, PIN numbers, account numbers, (including savings, checking, single-purpose and major credit cards, WIC, Family First, and Food Stamps) lawsuit case file numbers, equipment part numbers, (including automotive, electronic, plumbing, electrical, carpentry, etc.) serial numbers, "numbers" numbers, (such as Lotto, Mega Millions, Power Ball, King Kong Millions, Lucky 7s, Scratch & Match, Scratch & Win, Pick 4, Pick 6, Mega Ball, Bada Bling, etc.) and home security codes have all been changed, not to protect the cellophiles' privacy, (remember, they made their business public) but for the sole purpose of protecting the author against litigation.

Attention, passengers, this is the Commutication local to Final Thoughts, making the following station stops:

To make your trip more pleasant, we ask that you do not skip pages or chapters. Please do not leave this book unattended. It is a good book. Someone will find it and probably keep it, even if you provide return information on one of the pages. If this book is returned, it may not occur until after the finder has had a chance to read it.

If you recognize your conversation in this book, do not jump to the conclusion that your privacy was invaded. You advertised your end of the conversation for everyone to hear. To use the urban vernacular, you "put your business in the street." Just take comfort in the fact that your real name was not used.

Once again, this is the Commutication local to Final Thoughts. Please have all tickets out.

# How It All started

I was riding the 8:39PM Morris & Essex Line to Hoboken when a man sitting behind me was complaining about someone who was staying at his place "temporarily". He sounded like Steven Wright, a stand-up comic/actor who is known for his deadpan performances. I found it impossible to tune him out and was trying desperately to keep from laughing. You should have heard him!

MaOA6a:    I don't wanna give him money.
Because if I give him money, he's only gonna take the money and buy beer.
Now, if you wanna give him money, you can give him money.
But I don't wanna give him money. Because he's only gonna take the money and buy beer.
I don't understand why you would wanna give him money.
Well, I'm not gonna give him money. Because he's only gonna take the money and buy beer.

Ad infinitum / nauseam.

# What Do We Call Them?

Sifting through the countless possible names for these creatures was quite a task. After careful consideration, I was left with these options:

1. Cells – Way too basic

2. Cellolites
   Cellophites
   Celloses – These names would have been interesting...if they
             were characters in the Bible.

3. Celluloids
   Cellusians
   Celludians – Catchy, but a little too Sci-Fi.

4. Cellophants – This one was cool, but it sounds too much like
                "elephants".

5. Cellors – A homonym of "cellar", which is, "a room below
            ground level in a house." It could also suggest "one
            who occupies an intellectual and/or moral plane
            below the 'ground level' of acceptable behavior". Or
            "sellers" because they are trying to sell snippets of
            their lives to people who aren't interested.

6. Celluded – This was my favorite because it rhymes with
             "deluded". However, this one would only work as an
             adjective. It would also give the noun "celludians"
             more weight. So, I had to toss that one.

The names mentioned above did not cause people to cringe. I needed a name to represent an object of intense disdain. It had to be a name that no one would be proud to be called.

Then, it hit me...

# Glossary

cellophile

cel•lo•phile | ˌseləˈfīl |

noun
A person who speaks loudly while using a cellular phone in a public place, without consideration of his/her surroundings.

verb (cel•lo•phil•ing; **past** cel•lo•phil•ed) To speak loudly while using a cellular phone.

DERIVATIVES
cel•lo•phil•ic | selə'filik | adjective

cel•lo•phil•i•cal•ly | selə'filik (ə) lē | adverb

ORIGIN late 20th century. A fusion of two words:
from English, "cell", short for cellular phone.

ORIGIN from Greek –phile – loving
combining form (in this case) denoting fondness for a particularly vile act e.g. pedophile, necrophile, etc.

FaCM6l:   I still go to Lana.

Yeah, she has her own place in Madison.

And she has a girl there named Sally.

She is so awesome and she's such a
    sweetheart.

Sally is always so busy, so I usually spend about four
    hours in there just hanging out.

Yeah, bleach strips the color.

No.

I don't think you should color your hair.

You have enough color as it is.

Well, you don't wanna do too much.

Is it because Anthony likes her, or you just like her,
    too?

Really?

Yeah.

I think it would be good because you have a long face.

Yeah.

Right.

(laughs)

I didn't want that anymore!

It's just...

So you don't want to do it?

I don't want to get it too short!

So what's your sister's hair like?

No way!

Is it short?

Oh my God! Is it stylish?

Does she wear glasses?

Does it look really ridiculous?

She's around our age, like 25.

I used to work with this girl named Sarah, who was an in-line skater as well.

You know what?

Let me call you back.


Her phone rang moments later.


Yeah.

Let's do it around 7:00 or 7:30-ish.

Yeah.

I'll call you when I get out of here.

You're going to the mall?

My mother is going to Short Hills?

Yeah.

Just go there and relax.

Remember the calisthenics?

(laughs)

I could see that in a movie!

"The Bloomfields"!

I really don't know them that well.

Sounds good!

So, have a good workout!

Bye.


--------------------


MalC1t:   Where's IKEA?

Oh, I thought, 'You were coming all the way over there just to go to IKEA?'

I wish I lived closer to one.

That place rocks!

Yeah.

What consultants are you working with?

(laughs)

Speaking of French, John went to Montreal for Spring break, and Mom was saying if he got lost, to ask people where he was going in French.

He asked people in English and nobody understood what he was saying. So he asked one person how to get to

Melinda Street in French and he said, 'Yeah just go to the corner and make a left at the light and go down two blocks and you're there.

(laughs)

Yeah. It was pretty funny.

Yeah.

I'll talk to you.

--------------------

MaMS8g:   Hey, Mike.

How are you?

Sure.

I'm sure there'll be some kind of contract available. If you have any questions, call me. Otherwise, you can refer to the contract. OK?

I'll see you.

Bye.

--------------------

MaCM6o:   They might still do it, you know what I'm saying?

They was winning when I left.

I'm on the train now, so they might still do it.
   That's right.
That's right.
Gotta do what you gotta do.
Mmm-hmm.
Mmm-hmm. How was your Mother's Day? Yeah
   but, what I'ma do on Saturday is--
Yeah. I'm coming in the morning, too.
My church is sponsoring a bowling...


He got off the train.


--------------------


FcOA7u:  OK.

No.

I thought you were going to call me back!

OK!

When are you going to call me?

OK.

Bye.

--------------------

MaCM9w:  Hey.

Nothing.

Just calling to say "Hi".

Oh.

With who?

Oh, sweet.

No.

Actually, I'm not.

I'm on the train.

So, is she still sunburned?

Oh yeah.

I'm sorry.

Oh, OK.

That's cool.

But--

Yeah.

Ah...ouch!

Oh.

Who?

Yeah.

You sure?

You don't know these people.

Oh.

Yeah.

My friend.

Five?

Jeez!

Oh my God!

And who's paying for that?

Her parents?

That's awful!

Why are you at the mall in the first place?

I thought you wanted to go Sunday.

Hello?

Oh, no.

We...went...in...a...tunnel. So I may have to call
    you back.

Can you still hear me?

Hey. Sorry about that.

OK.

Me too.

Hold on. I...think...I...have...a...phone...call.

OK. I'll...see...you...soon.

He answered the other call.

    Hey, man. What's up?
    I should be home in twenty-five.
    No. Who—
    Who—
    Who—
    Who would you like to go mini-golfing with?
    OK.
    Yeah.

He dialed again...

    Hey!
    Hey...this...is...Alex.
    Hey.
    Oh.
    Going home from the city.
    It's OK. Thanks for asking.
    It's a camp in Maine.
    Wigwam.
    Peace.

and dialed again...

    Mike.
    Mike.
    Mike.
    I can swing it.

No.

No.

No.

We can rent a car, drive up. It'll be good.

Mike.

Mike, it's **not** insane.

How about this...I'll rent a car.

No.

No, it's no big deal.

OK.

and yet again...

> Hey. It's Alex Penn. I was calling to say "Hi." When
> you get this message, give me a call on my cell
> phone. I think you still have it. If you don't, it's
> xxx-xxxx. I hope everything's good with you.

and again...

> Hey. It's Alex Penn. I was calling to say "Hi." When
> you get this message, give me a call on my cell
> phone. I think you still have it. If you don't,
> it's xxx-xxxx. I hope everything's good with you.

and again.

> It is like, nine o'clock. You can call me...when...you...
> get...a...chance. I was in the city today. I hope things
> are good with you. Peace.

--------------------

FaCM2z:   Hi, Maria! It's Donna!
          How are you?
          I'm on my cell phone!
          I'm gonna be free in about two hours, OK?
          OK, bye!

--------------------

FcCM3h:   Hello.
          Hi.
          Nothing.
          On the train.
          I'm in Hoboken.
          Daddy?
          We all got really cool shoes!
          They were five dollars!
          It's on that pink sheet of paper.
          OK.
          I love you!
          Bye!

She dialed.

          Hello.
          Hi, Susan.
          We're on the train.
          Kayla, Mindy, Megan and Tiffany.
          I was walking around and I had no idea where
              north was!
          Then I found it and I was like, now which way do I go?
          You're with what's-his-name?

OK.
I'll be home by ten.
OK.
Bye.

--------------------

FaVA5k:  Yeah.
Hi.
On the train.
Yeah, and it's taking forever and she's being a pain in
the ass.
Hello?
Hello?
My phone's going out.
Hello?
Hello?
Wednesday night?
I know them very well.
I know who can get things signed.
She said you need to come to Vermont.
You need to relax.
She's pushing her mid 40s.
Ken is in his 30s.
There wouldn't be a government program if it was for
just us.
Yeah.
Bye.

--------------------

FaCM8m:  Hi, Amy. It's Kate.

I just wanted to confirm our plans.
Now, I just wanna make sure. You can handle the both
   of us?
OK.
Linda's threatening to come with us.
Don't worry.
(laughs)
We'll bring our own snacks!
(laughs loudly)
We won't eat you out of house and home!
Yeah.
Seattle, flight 78. Wednesday, the 9th.
I have to be back on the 14th.

PASSENGER: This is really pissing me off!

He got up quickly and proceeded toward the cellophile.

PASSENGER: I'm gonna to tell this woman...

He walked past her and entered another car. He reappeared
moments later and returned to his seat.

FaCM8m:    I think she only feels that way about some
               houseguests.
            (laughs loudly)
            Not you.
            No, not you!
            And we can take a cab!
            Yeah!
            It's important to know both ways!
            What?

Oh really?

Oh boy!

If you point me in the right direction!

(laughs loudly)

OK!

OK!

Oh, how nice!

(laughs loudly)

Very nice man!

Is that at cocktail hour?

Happy hour!

So, what's new and exciting?

Well, nothing much going on in the world of golf.

We're going to be playing—

PASSENGER: Shhhh!

Yeah.

It doesn't make it any worse.

It's good exercise.

Yeah.

Another thing is he's walking around the golf course.

He walks, so it's good exercise.

Yeah.

It's very annoying.

It does nothing for me.

That's true.

You could.

Well--

That's right!

Happy B-day to Frank!

It was on Sunday?

Happy belated!

Did you have a nice one?

Oh, how fun!

Oh, really?

(laughs)

It's the real thing!

Yeah, he wasn't my favorite!

Yeah, we're looking forward to it!

(laughs)

I can understand that!

Sounds like a good deal!

Good talking to you!

Yes!

(laughs)

I'll remember that one!

OK.

(laughs)

Maybe I'll get a chance to see that movie!

Well, it's a short story long!

I will make sure we get the best fares!

I'll check when I get home!

Yeah, me too!

Well, enjoy!

It's the least I could do!

OK, bye!

While on the train, please be courteous with your cell phone.

--AT&T billboard

# Index

The tag below shows how each cellophile was logged in my journal.

Example: MaBS5m

M **M**ale
F **F**emale
a **a**dult
c **c**hild

Species - **BS** – **B**ig**S**hot
           **CM** – **C**rass**M**ole
           **HR** – **H**ood**R**at
           **SB** – **S**ocial **B**utterfly
           **VA** – **V**oiceover **A**rtist
           **FC** – **F**oreign **C**opycat
           **MS** – **M**over/**S**haker
           **IE** – **I**d**le** Chatter
           **IO** – **I**d**o**l Chatter
           **OA** – **O**ver**A**ctor
           **EX** – **Ex**cusable
           **TC** – **T**rain **C**onductor
           5m – Tag number

MaCM4t: Hello?

Are you at the "punk" show?

It was OK.

I was supposed to talk about the Merrill proposal but
I talk about what I want.

It irritates my boss, but I don't care.

I want it, but I don't want the responsibility.

I just want to be known as #1, which I am apparently.

I don't wanna do the political stuff.

I just wanna have some fun.

That's new, "punk" music?

Oh. Well, have fun at the "punk" show.

Bye.

--------------------

FaOA9n: Hello?

I assumed your phone was turned off.

Why didn't you answer it?

Are you supposed to be there at ten in the morning?

To voice their satisfaction?

Oh, no.

Yes.

No, I'm not. I'm on the train right now.

I'm en route.

So it's probably for the best.

Umm, like working till the morning.

So, what should we do tomorrow?

I thought you were going to be off tomorrow.

I thought I was going to be off tomorrow, too.

So, Saturday and Sunday are out?

What about Monday?

And what's more important than my trip?

Do you think we should call?

You're sure you're not working on Friday after
    those meetings?

Or if I'm there Friday, I can go to Long Island.

Drop me off someplace.

Umm, which town is it in again?

Which town is it in again?

Isn't that right across the street from the giant
Roosevelt Field?

I grew up there! I love it there!

And also Eisenhower Park is there. I'd love to
    just walk around!

OK! OK!

--------------------

FaCM2u:   Hi, Macy!

I'm on the train in Hoboken!

I'm sitting on the train!

I'm sitting on the train in Hoboken station!

I'm on the train my daddy used to ride as a toddler!

Yeah!

I was in Manhattan!

Now I'm in Hoboken!

At the train station!

I get around!

Are you still fantasizing about me and the Saudi
Arabia?

Yeah!

Mon is good!

Mon is good!

Mon is good!

He is the custodian of the holy place!

He is the custodian of the holy place!

He is the custodian of the holy place!

It's the holiest place on the world!

Muslims say it's theirs, Israelis say it's theirs!

Holy place!

I'm in the best seat!

I'm in the captain's seat!

The train is about to leave!

You get overtime?

Time and a half!

Once in a while I'd get triple time!

That's rare!

I'd get 300!

I talked to the rabbis!

They're my best friend!

They handled my orthodontist to make my teeth
   straight!

I wanted to do it for any homeless families!

Now, I just want to give it to the Jewish boys!

I changed it!

No one saw the note for the homeless families!

The homeless families missed the boat!

They won't have to worry about paying the $250!

It'll be Boys Town!

The train's rolling now!

I gotta watch this!

She scurried to another window.

You could talk while I'm watching!
I have a Pakistani!
Big, gigantic bodyguard!
Big!
Big!
Big!
I don't want the neighbors to see the license
    plates!
He'll have no problem lifting big trunks!
I'll just treat him to hamburgers at McDonald's!
Yeah!
Then take him back to EXXON!
This is exciting!
I can still see Hoboken!
My dad used to come here!
They might want to rape her or cut her throat!
I can do it in—this is exciting!
I can see the Empire State building!
Daddy used to come to Hoboken in the '40s!
He worked on the trains!
That's when he met Mommy!
That's when I was spat out!
If they ask about siblings, I won't discuss it!
I don't want them to know that I have siblings!
I cover everything!
I'm talking loud for the whole train car to hear!
What did you say, Macy?
What did you say, Macy?
What did you say, Macy?
Hello?
Hello?

Macy?

Macy?

(laughs loudly)

I know it sounds like movie folks!

I hope I didn't miss my stop!

I went to a job interview and--

Hello?

Hello?

OK. They didn't get to the first stop!

I'm looking out the window!

I thought we were heading out to the country or like

Pennsylvania or something!

The only thing going out to the country is what?

I wanted to tell you something!

Are you there, Macy?

Are you there, Macy?

My mother has a CD and I can't touch it!

My mother has a CD and I can't touch it!

He said if I bottom out, I'm on my own!

She scampered to another window.

Aw man, this is exciting!

I'm sitting in the car!

A job I might take, I'll need the car!

One, I need the train, they said!

They said, "Consider yourself hired!"

"You'll be working for us!"

You know what they did?

They said, "Consider yourself working for us!"

The one you married!

They do something wrong and they see a doctor!

Take pills and they are!

My brother did what you did!

And that's when I told him to do what I told you to do!

Did you explain to him that you were fantasizing
about me and the Saudi Arabia?

I thought that's what you would have told him!

I'm listening to you!

Shipping in Hasbrouck Heights!

We just passed the choo-choo train station!

Then we went to Manhattan and then we went back
to Hoboken!

I had to use the ticket where the car is!

Hertz hired me in Newark!

Newark hired me!

Newark is the biggest city in the state!

And Port Newark is Newark!

Hertz is in Hoboken but they hired me in
Newark!

So, the biggest city in the state hired me!

She hobbled off at Newark Broad Street.

--------------------

MaMS1g:   I got a new client.
          ECO 12.
          You know what that means?
          I'm on the train.
          I'm on the train.
          Let's face it, that's about as much as I spend, so it
              works out.
          If I did that, then I'd be sleeping in first class!

(laughs)

You know what they give you in first class?

As much free alcohol as you want!

(laughs)

They don't mess around anymore!

I should call who?

Sandy?

Yeah, you're right if that's the case!

Ask her if she has any inside info!

Ask her.

Tell her I'm curious if she has any inside info.

Tap her and ask her!

How did I do in Vegas?

Laid out by the pool!

The trip was paid for, not by me!

I won about $175.00!

I figured out the wheel and I started winning!

They were serving me up too!

Pardon me?

Yeah, I didn't pay for anything.

That sucks.

I said earlier.

(laughs)

It's a keeper.

So, Arnold's friendly government wasn't impressed with Term 3?

He had three lines.

I'll be back.

(pause)

I'm back.

No, you're not getting off that easy!

No, you're not!

I want you to ask your wife.

How does she know that I'm going to pay for it?

Ask her!

You're kidding!

Wow!

What's that?

Brandon, I need to get with Rick and get a free plane
    ride!

She told the difference between her and her husband?

He ranked a 4 and she went 24-and-a-half!

(laughs loudly)

Does that sound like something he would say?

Give that good man a free ride home!

I learned from the best!

How funny was that when I hit him?

I wouldn't get away with that at the door!

I gotta get going!

--------------------

MaCM0z:    Hi, James, it's Mr. Diamond.

    Alex Diamond.

    Alexander Diamond.

    OK, I can talk to him later.

    D-I-A-M-O-N-D.

    My phone number is xxx-xxxx.

    D-I-A-M-O-N-D-.

    My phone number is xxx-xxxx.

    OK, bye.

He dialed.

    Hi Michael, it's Alex Diamond. It's 10:15. I talked to
    Fred. We made an appointment at 9:00 to meet
    with the union. I'd really appreciate you attending
    the meeting and I appreciate your commitment.

--------------------

FaCM7m: Hey, Jennie!
Yeah!
You already told me!
Oh, really?
I really liked them!
So, I'm like, really pleased with the shoes!
They're like, old clearance!
I know you don't know the return policy!
They're like, a loafer with no backing!
They're black with white stitching!
Yeah!
At first, I found them, like, on the floor!
You have to try them on before you buy them!
She was so mean!
So, I tried them on and they were good!
Then I had to--
Yeah!
Then I saw this, like, caramel pair!
Umm, I thought they were cute. Then I thought
about how much I'd wear them!
Like, I couldn't wear them to work!
I could, but they have flowers!
It was really crazy!

Suddenly, the cellophile realized she was talking loudly, so she lowered her voice.

--------------------

MalE9q: You're a loser!

30

We're on the train.
We're on the train
(sings "Locomotion")
You have two more?
What could take you six hours?
Are you going to Mom and Dad's?
You're going to a movie?
We haven't been to a movie.
No!
Some kids are laughing.
(to his travel companion) He asked if someone is
    barking on the train.
Dogs go "mooooo!"
I'm going to set my alarm clock.
So I'll call you when I get up.
How about you call **me** when **you** get up?
I'll be on the road.
**Where** I'm going to be on the road is another
    question!
Sunday I'm leaving at ten, so you need to bring me
    back at ten.
OK?
I could really leave at twelve.
So I can have lunch with your mom.
I think we should get tickets because the game is
    going to end early.
I like the way you think!
I'm going to go the bathroom!

He got up and proceeded toward the end of the car.

I could take you with me, but I'm gonna hang up.

If you love your cell phone so much, why are you yelling at it?

-- AT&T billboard

# CrassMole (rhymes with...)

This species represents the majority of cellophiles, which feeds on the events of its life with a bit more enthusiasm than is warranted. Its dry, matted fur consists of countless details of its life, all of which are unimportant.

When the CrassMole talks, it rubs its jagged teeth across its tongue, producing the sound of rusty nails scraping a chalkboard, pieces of Styrofoam rubbing together, or any other cringe-inducing sound, which is sure to irritate everyone within earshot.

Another annoying trait of the CrassMole is that it carries itself with a sense of entitlement, as if it doesn't have to adhere to the standards of decent behavior, while expecting others to obey said rules. All cellophiles possess this characteristic, but on the CrassMole, it forms a visible layer of viscous slime that smells like urine from someone who doesn't drink enough water. Its dead skin cells and shed hair can be seen trapped in the goo.

MaCM8y:   Hi, Eileen!

How are my buddies?

Did they have a good dinner?

Well, we're on the train!

OK, we'll see you later!


She dialed.


Hi, Miss Janet!

Kevin says "Hi!"

(to Kevin) Say "Hi."

We're on New Jersey Transit!

We went to Dana's!

Don't worry!

No...uh, today?

Yeah!

Did she say anything at all?

Yeah, I hear you, Janet!

Can you hear me?

Greg will just tell us.

Yeah!

Yeah, I'm listening!

Mmmm.

Really?

A liar's a liar!

She's being extremely evasive!

I mean you heard what I said!

Well, what were you thinking?

So, what can I do?

I have not told any of that!

So, this isn't about us?
But how could they not follow up on this business?
Hmmm.
Do you think it could be true?
You can have it good! You can have it bad!
The car service?
I didn't call him back, but apparently—
(laughs)
Yeah!
Well, why aren't you communicating?
I just wanna stay in business!
(laughs)
It's too funny!
OK!
Bye!

--------------------

FalE4b:    Hey!
           How are you?
           On the train.
           You're home?
           How long are you staying?
           No, I'm going to a meeting for my class next week.
           So, I don't know if I should go there, then go back
               with you on—
           Yeah, Friday.
           That's what they said.
           You're pushing it.
           Yeah.
           Uh-huh.
           (laughs)
           OK.

What is he doing?

Oh, he's looking for a job.

It's difficult.

So, how's law school, girl?

I can't believe you're in law school!

It's so ridiculous!

It's so ridiculous!

Your problem is law school?

Oh, but it's more liberal than other law schools?

You know how we do.

Yeah.

You'll be cramming every day.

Uh-huh.

(laughs)

They're OK.

Yeah.

And that's the thing.

Everybody has, like, a "thing".

It's like, I was thinking about the sociology but I didn't
    want to do that.

Yeah, but that makes all the difference in the world.

Because you come home to nothing.

That's good.

And I wish he would come up, but it's all good.

I call him "Fella."

That's what his mother calls him.

All his people call him that.


She got off the train.


--------------------

FaCM6r:   Hello?

Wake up!

Where were you?

I'm gonna quit.

Yeah.

Huh?

Maybe they can see you.

No plans.

No plans.

So bad!

Well, you might be lazy!

Oh, great!

Brooklyn's not an hour away!

Yeah.

I'm closer to you than she is.

Why not?

Say it!

Right now I can't!

I can't do it!

I have self-respect!

I do!

You tryin' to be a playa!

What you sayin' don't make sense!

I don't know what I was gonna say!

Oh, you are great!

This was my stop.

--------------------

MaCM0m:   Hey, dude.

How'd your day with Joe go?

How'd your day with Joe go?

Oh yeah?

That's not good if it doesn't work.

Well, don't tell me!

(laughs)

What was this one for, a teacher?

What was this one for, a teacher?

Well, you ought to know better.

Well, you ought to know better.

Well, you might be able to repair it.

Is that what you're telling me about?

"The fireman and the Indian?"

Yeah.

I'm on the 8:46.

I missed the last one.

I know they ran a couple of them close together.

In the dark?

Yeah, well.

Nah, I'll just go to the bar and have a beer.

The kids have been off.

They're off tomorrow, too

Yeah, it's some teacher conference or something.

Yeah, I'll bet they're spending that money as fast as they
make it.

(laughs)

I don't know how close I am to that one.

Yeah, maybe the Road Show.

The weather's been all fucked up.

What?

Yeah, we'll walk.

We'll do something.

There's a lot of them to see.

Yeah, the fish alone will keep them going.

I was bored shitless.

(laughs)

The only thing he wanted to do was ride home.

It was the best part of my day.

I put him on a train.

Well, maybe I'll take him to Coney Island or
something.

I'll talk to you later.

I'm gonna lose you.

--------------------

MalE2v:   You can't believe how cold it is!

You can't believe how cold it is!

It's not supposed to get any higher than 22 degrees!

Did you get a Washington Post?

No. Get a Post.

Yeah.

It should be a front-page story.

Oh well, good for both of them.

All right.

What time is it supposed to start?

All right.

You got it.

He dialed again.

Hi, Jen.

What you doin'?

Why are you at home?

What happened?

You don't know?

(laughs)

Oh, you got report cards?

So, you got a three-day weekend?

You had Martin Luther King?

Oh.

No, that was Monday.

Whose birthday is it now?

So, you had Monday and Friday?

Good week!

Where's your brother?

Hi, Sonny.

How you doin'?

You all packed up?

I can't hear you, son.

You sure you're OK to drive?

I can't hear you.

Well, call me when you get there.

Did you get your schedule?

What do you got?

Calculus?

Rehab?

Some program? Or something else?

Anybody else?

Or is it just you?

Apprentice program?

Opportunities in Washington?

Y'all need to drop that quarterback.

Y'all need to drop that receiver, too.

Stop eatin' so much of that cake and shit!

All right.

MaSB7w:  I could come in at 7:00 in the morning.
Monday and Tuesday.
I'm busy till 6:00.
Uh...I just thought about it.
Yeah, you might want to do that.
OK.
Uh...hopefully for the summer I could—
Oh, yes!
That would be great!
OK.
Yep.
Yep.
OK.
For this job, is he going into the summer?
Oh, really?
Oh, OK.
OK.
I guess he was on the shore.
Oh yeah.
Yes.
OK.
All right.
Have you ever heard of that commercial?
I don't know.
I have no idea.
It goes so many different ways.
Are you on the computer today?
What kind of games I like to play?
Usually fact games.
OK.
Bye.

# HoodRat

The HoodRat comes in a variety of shapes, sizes and ethnicities. It only adorns its shallow hide with name-brand designs.

The HoodRat carries itself with a rather antagonistic demeanor. With stiff bristles that always seem to stand on end, it usually intimidates those who are not familiar with the breed. While it is approachable, it is not wise to admonish the species about its cell phone use. Criticizing other aspects of its behavior could also be risky, for it will bear its sharp teeth and retractable claws at the first sign of danger. But like the Big Shot, the HoodRat's conversations can provide an entertaining glimpse into its way of life.

FaSB9j: Hello.

How are you doing?

I'm fine!

Yeah, I did! Thank you so much!

(laughs)

Oh, we're so funny!

That was so sweet! Thank you!

I know! You are so wise! Thank you so much!

You can tell him!

Aw gee, yeah!

Like, no way! Thank you!

I know!

Oh, that's right!

Oh wow!

That's so true!

Oh definitely!

That was a major beef with my friend!

Definitely! I know!

I know!

Thank you!

Aaaawww!

That's so cute!

I get mad!

I scream and yell!

Can you hear me?

I know! It's so hard, right?

Right!

Right!

Why, thank you! You're so supportive!

I know!

Right!

Everyone is narrow-minded!

I know!
Wow!
Thank you! I appreciate it!
Have so much fun!
Can you hear me?
If you can hear me, have so much fun!
Have a good evening!
Bye!

--------------------

FaCM5p:   Oh shit!
(laughs)
I'm hoping I could get off.
(laughs)
I'm really excited!
Oh my God!
You totally do!
I have to remember to bring my typewriter so I might
   get some work!
(laughs)
Fifteen hours, that's a lot!
Oh my God!
I'm really gonna do something for the kids.
Yeah, like, the kids are crying.
(laughs)
Mm-hmm.
(laughs)
Whatever.
Well, don't.
Come on!

I'm going to be here for a while and there are no clubs!
(laughs)
That makes sense.
That makes sense.
 (laughs)
Yeah, like he had his fun!
Yeah, like every mall for the rest of their lives.
I have to be in South Orange.
No.
I rarely date boys.
I was like—


We entered a tunnel.


Hello?
Stop.
Every time I think about it.
All those thousands and thousands I saved.
It was talking about all this stuff is like damnation
    to women.
It was a total feminist drag.
So, we were chatting.
(laughs)
I'm just saying.
Yes!
Yes!
Oh my God!
That's so funny!
That's so funny!
Yeah.
Yeah.
Yeah.

Really?

(laughs)

Mm-hmm.

Yeah.

Isn't that about to close down?

That's so sad!

Really?

Wow!

Yeah.

It can't be like college.

I mean it can't be like high school.

It only had 850 students.

It only had 850 students in the whole university.

I know, but just for conversation sake.

I'm not trying to hate!

I'm serious!

They're like, on two different tiers!

No!

No!

No!

No!

You talk about structure.

I'm serious!

There's no comparison!

It's a lot higher as far as education is concerned.

Yeah!

Yeah!

It's focused on teaching than publishing because you know you would have been ignored the entire four years.

They're not under in terms of institution, but in terms of publishing--

Yeah!

You see what I'm saying?

No.

No.

No.

No.

Yeah, you're right.

I never thought about that too.

Are you kidding me?

(laughs)

Wow!

Mm-hmm.

But I love it!

But I love it!

Yeah!

Well, they charge about a dollar an hour.

(laughs)

Oh, that's so funny!

What?

Isn't she in her third year?

I think she's in her third year.

'Cause if you did, we can't hang out!

'Cause if you did, we can't hang out!

(laughs)

I know you that well!

Oh my God!

Seriously!

I got all the winners!

All the winners, all the time.

Um, you're right.

You're right.

You're right.

You're -

You're college-ish.

(laughs)

I would have to take it down.

What?

It's just that there are better women out there than
    there are men.

Mm-hmm.

Exactly!

You know it.

They be like, "Who's that stink guy?"

(laughs)

I adore the people.

(laughs)

(giggles)

(more giggling)


This was my stop.


--------------------


MaCM3t:    Hi.

Did she call?

What did she say?

How am I?

Medically or psychologically?

Medically, I'm fine. Psychologically, I'm concerned.

I'm on the train, going to the city.

No, I didn't sleep well last night.

It's possible.

It's possible.

Right.

Right.

You know, I gotta tell you. I don't know what the
    prospects are.

If it doesn't spread I'm gonna be concerned, but if it does
I'm gonna be good.
Yeah.
I know.
OK.
Bye.

He dialed again.

Hello?
Is Marla there?
Is Marla there?
Hello?

Moments later…

Hello?
Is Marla there?
Is Marla there?
Jim.
Anthony's father.
I'm, Anthony's father.
Yes. Anthony fell today and landed on his head and I just
wanted to tell you he's OK.
I know you're really super busy.
I just wanted to let you know.

He got up and entered the vestibule while dialing a number. It
would have been nice if he had remembered to keep his voice
down.

Hello?
Is Marla there?
Is Marla there?

Jim.

Anthony's father.

Yes!

Hi.

Yes.

Anthony fell and landed on his head.

Yes, he's OK.

I just wanted you to keep an eye on him.

Yes.

It's OK for him to go to sleep.

He can go to sleep if he's tired.

Just keep an eye on him, OK?

Oh my goodness!

Yes.

Thank you.

Bye.

--------------------

MaOA1e:   Hello?

OK, sweetie.

Are you on the train?

OK, when does the show end?

Are you coming home right after the show?

When the show is over, call us and tell us.

Call us immediately after the show.

Because I don't want it to be one of those things
where you get out and don't come home right
after.

Are you coming right after the show?

Then it's not right away!

If you're not coming home immediately after

the show you need to tell me!
What time are you going to be home?
No! No! No! No! No! Tell me what time you're
   going to be home!
Yes!
OK but don't ever do this again!
I-I-I guess, Elaine, but you're really putting me on the spot!
Now you can explain to me!
I know her dad!
You're going to where?
Is it a play or a movie?
What time does the show begin?
OK!
All right, sweetie, don't come down the spotlight side!
You can't put us on the spot like this again!
Talk to Mom!
Definitely call Mom!

--------------------

FaCM3x:   So I finally gave up and called twice.
And I'm like, 'Why am I calling?'
It doesn't even make sense for **me** to call.
She's like, 'None of you really know him.'
Do you think you could physically describe him?
And she's like, 'Does he sound cute?'
I don't know.
And she's like, 'He's a tall redhead.'
And then she started asking me about his family and
I'm like...
So, this is what I told him
I said there's two things.

Or you can get into it and there's a chance you can get let
   down.
He left this dumb message like, 'I had a great time. Have a
   good day.'
He's not even like a normal boyfriend, not even distinctive,
   and I'm like, 'Whatever.'
Mm-hmm.
Mm-hmm.
That's what he is.
Mm-hmm.
OK.
Talk to you soon.

---------------------

FaCM4g:    Because that's all I want.
           Yeah.
           I don't know why.
           But I will surely know soon.
           Oh my God!
           Whaaaat?
           (laughs)
           We're having an uprising because women are getting
              really aggressive lately.
           Right.
           Right.
           Right.
           (laughs)
           Mm-hmm.
           Mm-hmm.
           Oh.
           Oh.

She coming down.

To the mulch!

(laughs)

Don't cause my boy to take that acid pill today!

(laughs)

Mm-hmm.

Oh my God!

Mm-hmm.

Mm-hmm.

Right!

Right!

Right!

That's good!

That's right!

OK.

Mm-hmm.

Mm-hmm.

Mm-hmm.

(laughs)

Here, here, here. G-A-L Get a life!

Get a life!

Get a life!

Mm-hmm!

Mm-hmm!

Mm-hmm!

(laughs)

FaCM4g:   Isn't that evil?

You are all so evil!

But it's good!

I know he was glad I wasn't in the office!

I know he was like, 'Thank God!'

Noooo!

(laughs)

Y'all been doin' that all the time!

Right!

Oh my God!

Oooooh!

Uh-huh.

Mm-hmm.

Right.

(laughs)

You're evil!

You're evil!

Yes!

Yes!

All right!

(laughs)

That's right.

What's up with your man?

I don't know!

I know that's your man!

Go play with Andrew.

I'll talk to you tomorrow.

--------------------

MaCM8p:  Hi. How are you?

No.

Did you talk to your parents?

No.

On the train.

Did you talk to your aunt?

How's she?

Anyone else call?

No one.

Oh yeah?

I'm sad that he's coming.

I talked to Mom and she said, 'I don't wanna talk to him',
    and I left it at that.

Really?

He put a bid on the house.

I told him that he could get us the best rate.

OK.

Well, I'll talk to you, OK?

Bye.

--------------------

MaVA6d:     All this terrorism stuff is crazy.

And the scary thing is that they put God behind it.

In his speech he says he's an Evangelical Christian.

I just have to go through a tunnel...

Are you still there?

--------------------

MaOA0b:     Will you shut up?

Don't believe the rumors!

Because I said so!

So what!

Don't believe the fucking rumors!

Hello?

Hello?

--------------------

MaOA6w:     Barbara, you don't call. You don't write.
            This is Mark.
            OK.
            All right.
            Bye.


His phone rang.


            I was expecting to hear from you a little sooner.
            I didn't think I had to track you down.
            How you been?
            Yeah?
            What was it?
            I went to DC.
            It seems so far from that weekend.
            A lot of breakdowns in the real world, let's put it that
                way.
            It always seemed to work well for me when I'm
                there...
            Hello?
            Hello?


                    --------------------


FaHR1y:     So I just started ignoring her. And she started leaving
                all kinds of nasty messages.
            Yeah. I have to call my mom.
            OK.
            I'll give you a call when I get there.
            OK, bye.

                    --------------------

MaOA2n:    Hello?

Yeah.

I'm sorry.

(sounding irritated) I couldn't understand what
you said!

What's the number on the bottom of the envelope?

What's that?

Yeah.

(still irritated) Then you should!

I'm almost there!

I'll call you when I get there!

OK!

(even more irritated) Iloveyoubye!

--------------------

MaCM7o:    Yeah.

Yeah.

I think he was cheating on her.

They don't know anything.

Ken doesn't communicate.

And Barbara...

She's recovering forever.

Can you hear me?

I'm surprised because I'm in a tunnel, we don't lose
each other.

Once we're out of the tunnel, we lose each other.

Who's picking up Jerry?

Who's picking up Jerry in a taxi?

OK.

All right.

I'll see you later, then.

Bye.

# Monkey See...

The need to cellophile is contagious. When one sees or hears another talking, he/she is compelled to reach for the phone, dial a number and talk to someone, anyone, about absolutely nothing. How do I know? I've done it myself. Yes, I was once a cellophile, too! I remember walking the streets of New York on my way to work and after seeing another cellophile engaged in unimportant banter, I felt an uncontrollable urge to whip out my cell and call a friend. The conversation went something like this:

ME:  Hey, Louie!
     What are you doing?
     I'm on my way to work.
     I'm walking down 33rd now.
     Yeah.
     All right.
     I'll talk to you later.

A wave of exuberance washed over me immediately. A wide, goofy smile spread itself across my face like cream cheese on an everything bagel. My walk morphed into a swagger. Now I was hip, a member of an exclusive club of the "connected". To an imaginary camera, I flashed my Kool-Aid grin while giving a thumbs-up. A gesture that said, "I'm in!"

It was so stupid.

I was in a restaurant with a friend one Saturday afternoon. While we were waiting our turn for service, he whipped out his little electronic friend, dialed and proceeded to talk about nothing.

Well, the woman at the next table would not be outdone. I noticed her looking at my friend's phone while pulling out hers, opening it very slowly, with the display facing us so that we--and anyone who was interested or not--could see that she had the same model as my friend's. She pressed a few buttons and put it to her ear and listened for all of thirty seconds. Then, she closed the device and returned it to her purse.

Try it. Pull out your phone and start dialing, put it to your ear and look around. I guarantee your actions will inspire others to do the same.

FaOA5t: Well, she said that I'm too nice, too trusting and too
"go along."
And it doesn't look good with guys.
No, not "God". "Guys". With men.
Well, I can't be anything but who I am.
Yeah.
(pause)
Hi.
You're so sweet, baby.
So, Mommy will call you.
Put her back on.
I don't know. Probably go home and sleep.
I wanted to go out but the person I was going to go out
with called to go to work.
No.
I said it's the second day on my job.
No, I didn't put "305".
I put "301".
Oh my goodness!
I said to Kate I was sending it to 301!
301!
And she didn't correct me then!
I'll trace it today!
I can't trace it as soon as I get to work but I'll trace it
today!
And you know, Ma, I knew it was 301!
I used to be good at remembering numbers!
OK. I'll trace it.
I'll call you back.

--------------------

FaCM1k:   Our flight is on Saturday.

Yeah. The doctor wants to see her on Tuesday.

I know it's a big imposition on you.

Well, he said that she has bumps on her throat and—
(train conductor makes an announcement)
So we go to Seattle on Saturday.

She dialed again...

Hi, Dad.

All right. How are you?

She's sick.

She's had chest X-rays and blood work.

So, we're going to Seattle on Saturday and we're
going to the doctor on Tuesday.

Yeah. So, what's the scoop?

She has to go to an internist and she's going to take
extensive steroids like candy.

She's gotta be on antibiotics.

Yeah. Have a glass of wine and chill out.

Well, I knew this was going to happen and I was
running around to all these doctors.

Yeah.

OK.

Thanks, Dad.

Talk to you.

Bye.

and again.

Hi. I'd like to place an order for pick-up.

Some sweet and sour.

A large won ton.

Beef strips and lamb and broccoli.

No, beef and broccoli.

My train doesn't get there till eighteen-after-nine, is that
OK?
OK.
Bye.

--------------------

MaOA0v:    Good morning.
           OK. How are you?
           Why you sound so sad?
           OK.
           OK.
           Well then, I won't call!
           Then, don't!

--------------------

FaOA5y:    I am a better person than you're perceiving me!
           But, honey, you have to understand!
           I had to find the train!
           I couldn't find the schedule!
           I thought you were going to take the train!
           You have to know that I care about you!
           I had to find the train!
           Hello?
           Hello?
           Hello?
           Are you there?
           Well, obviously you weren't listening to me this
               morning!
           Do you wanna get dinner?
           Do you wanna get sushi?

You can bring something from the refrigerator if you want.
OK.
Bye.

--------------------

FaOA7s:  I don't know, 20 pounds?
That's just annoying as hell!
He cost me a pretty penny!
OK.
Well, that should go back to the store!
They said they would!
Mmm-hmm.
Well, you know, try to put it back in the box or
    something.
No. We're supposed to be leaving any second now.
OK.
Bye.

--------------------

FaOA2m:  Are you dodging my calls?
On my cell phone!

She redialed.

Did you hang up on me?

PASSENGER:  "This is ridiculous!"

The passenger tried to go to the next car to the next car, but the door was locked. As he returned to his seat, he looked down at the cellophile in disgust. The cellophile must have caught his glare because she lowered her voice for the rest of the trip.

--------------------

FaBS8o:    Dora.

        Did I get any calls?

        I'm expecting a call from CVC.

        They called?

        They were supposed to tell me.

        It's a cell phone.

        xxx-xxxx.

        What's the number?

        The name is Darla?

She hung up and dialed.

        Hello, Darla?

        Did I call you or did I speak to Sister Small?

        Can you hold on?

        (pause)

        Hello?

        I got the letter about the pending audit.

        I got the letter about the policy and it said it had

            enclosures, but there were no enclosures.

        No, that's OK.

        I have a captive audience.

        I'm on the train.

        Ralph?

        It is addressed to Paul Kris, President of the Board of

Directors?

He is not!

All correspondence must be sent to my attention!

I am the President of the Board of Directors!

That's OK.

OK.

OK.

OK.

OK.

OK.

OK.

OK.

xxxx.

OK.

OK, thanks a lot.

She dialed again.

I'm on the train.

The Audit Manager told me to be on guard.

He wouldn't tell me that.

That is messed up.

Exactly.

Exactly.

Yeah, yeah, I hear you.

What?

You're breaking up.

She never tried to call the person back.

--------------------

MaMS0r:   Hi!
How are you?
I was able to get to a meeting.
Yeah.
Yeah.
What I did was—
My wife's mother—
She took some time off and she—
She's in the hospital and...

He got up and went to another car. That was nice.

--------------------

FaMS3p:   Hi.
How are you?
I'm fine.
Well, I'm on my way in Manhattan.
Well, Mom wanted to keep it to two minutes.
I stayed and I'll leave on Saturday.
We have visitation from 12:45 to 2:00.
We have a meeting with the doctor today and again
   on Saturday.
It truly is.
It really is.
On the outset, it was optimistic.
But on Sunday it was...
I'm on the train, so I can't get into specifics.
I'm going to try to e-mail everybody when I get more
   feedback.
OK.
Bye.

---------------------

Even train conductors can be cellophiles.

FaTC4z:    Who's watching the kids?
           Excuse me?
           Who left him in charge?
           Who left him in charge?
           Uh-huh.
           Michael is only eight!
           Good-bye.

She dialed another number but there was no answer. She hung
up and tried another.

           Hi.
           Call my house and find out why ain't nobody answerin'
                the phone!
           Uh-huh.
           Ain't nobody there?
           OK.
           Nobody's home?
           OK.
           OK.
           That's cool.
           Just checking on the house.
           Bye.

           ---------------------

MalE9v:    I'd like to have her as a friend.
           I'd like to have her as a friend but...

She says the right thing, but there was like a child behind
    it.
Yeah.
She warmed up a little.
So, I was like, whatever.
So, I have a five-year-plan with this girl.
I have a plan.
Yeah, definitely.
Maybe it's something she can't help.
Yeah.
Yeah.
Like a lot of other things, it needs care.
You saw him?
Oh.
Yeah.
Oh yeah, Nick.
Right.
Right.
Right.
Oh no!
Yeah.
Yeah.
Yeah.
I feel the exact same way.
I'm on the train.
Not my apartment.
In some ways it felt like a safety net.
Yeah.
Yeah.
To get a balance.
Staying down there wasn't something I wanted to do.
OK.

# BigShot

This breed is very sensitive to what others think of it, so it must present the illusion of success. The BigShot has big plans and wants everyone within earshot to know about them.

The B.S. takes special care in displaying only the most pristine sections of its broad and colorful plumage, which is usually modeled after business attire. A splash of something different – like a large fedora or a bright handkerchief – helps to establish this species as a nonconformist.

The B.S. loves attention, even if it draws the ire of its fellow passengers. It does not pause during the conductor's announcements, for its conversations are far more important than anything uttered over the public address system.

Its demeanor seems to dare anyone to interrupt it. But sometimes, its topics of discussion can be quite amusing. It is often difficult to discern whether humans are afraid to admonish it for talking so loudly, or if they are actually entertained by what the creature is saying. I must admit that I have participated in the latter assessment.

The BigShot is confident and loves to hear itself speak, regardless of grammatical errors, (perhaps another desire to go against the grain). It feeds on a steady diet of bragging and name-dropping. All of this verbal preening keeps its more attractive feathers shiny, while the dull ones are tucked underneath. It walks with its chest protruded forward. Its gait is usually punctuated by an exaggerated swing of the arms, accompanied by a dip of the shoulders and a deep limp, much like the "Jive Turkey", a species believed to have gone extinct after the 1970s.

MaVA6h:    My brother was so much into schedules and stuff.
           Yeah.
           Yeah.
           Yeah.
           Right.
           Oh, he told me a little about it.
           It's so sad.
           Oh my God!
           When I bring it up, she gets all riled up about it.
           Yeah.
           Yeah.
           I remember.
           Yeah.
           Yeah.
           He watches sports but it's not like he's all passionate
               about it.
           They fixed the blood problem.
           Getting blood clots is bad, isn't it?
           I don't know.
           I definitely do.
           I get tense from that.
           He thinks one of his friends from high school, like,
               gave him AIDS.
           I don't know.
           I don't know.
           I don't know if I can trust that.
           I remember that.
           Right now.
           They did it right now?
           Oh, they did it at college.
           Oh my God!

Yeah.

I'm gonna tell his grandmother.

All right.

--------------------

Fa8OAt:   OK, where's Stan?

Where is he?

Where is he?

OK.

What's your problem today?

OK.

Bye.

--------------------

FaHR4m:   Hello?

Nothin'. What's up with you?

Wait a minute!

How you gonna be callin' me, cursin' and barkin' at
     me?

I can't call you back!

I'm on the train, on my way home!

Listen! You need to grow up!

You need to grow up!

You don't call me cursin' and barkin' at me!

She hung up and dialed.

FaOA4m:   She calls me, cursin' at me, blah, blah, blah!

And she only call me when she need something!

You know, family members always do that!

And they treat you like shit all the other times!
And then when they need you, they call!
They treat you like some millionaire!
They don't know how to survive!
They don't know how you live!
They think you should always have something for them!
They don't consider that you have light bills to pay!
They don't consider that you have to have money for the
    bus to get to work!
And that's what she do!
I'm on the train.
All right.

--------------------

MaVA1q:    Although she doesn't know these things, someone
    should have told her.
So, she didn't acknowledge him at all? Is that what
    you're saying?
Uh-huh.
Uh-huh.
Uh-huh.
What was the other event?
Uh-huh.
Uh-huh.
Uh-huh.
Uh-huh.
Uh-huh.
Uh-huh.
Uh-huh.
Well, Sam, you know-
Hmmmm...

Uh-huh.

Right

Oh, I know.

No, I-

I-

Yeah, I-

I-

I get the drift.

Well she's-

No.

No.

No.

That is true that she fucked that up.

That's OK.

So she blames Kim.

She should have called.

I've called him at 2 o'clock in the morning.

No one knew she was going to say anything.

If she knew, she should have called someone else.

She had everybody's number.

And you're right.

If relationships were different-

It's not Margaret's job to do that.

Yes. I understand what you mean.

Yeah but, with Matt what's-his-name and Alex being the
    pain in the ass that he is-

I know the way the evidence presents itself makes the
    situation less serious than it really is.

Don Willis.

I wonder if he knows to acknowledge the understudy?

(laughs)

Oh, I hope this one does well.

No. You have to go back to your surroundings.

Believe me. I'm totally clear on it.

The thing is nobody knew she was going to say anything.

If she knew she was going to say something on "Good Morning America", then she should have talked to somebody.

Yeah, well, we'll go into it.

Thanks, Steve.

Talk to you soon.

--------------------

MaCM7i:    Hi. I'm calling for a cab to meet me at the Summit Station

About 9:30.

Is that too late?

Do you know of one who will?

Summit?

Thank you.

OK, bye.

He dialed another number.

Hello Maggie?

It's me.

Could you do me a favor?

Could you come and get me?

I could have taken a car service but...

He wouldn't give me a voucher.

But I got one.

But I'd rather not use it today.

Because he didn't give me one and I don't want him to go

checking to see if I used a service.

And I left early, too.

So, I don't want him to check what time I used it.

So, that's why I need you to...do me...a favor.

Are you sure?

OK.

Thanks.

I love you.

Bye.

--------------------

FaVA1c:   The taxi driver got me to Penn Station in ten minutes!

I had to make the train in twelve minutes!

I made it in about thirty seconds!

What's going on?

I'm still on the train.

Well, why don't you get escorted to your office?

Are they allowed to do that if it affects your
livelihood?

Are they allowed to do that if it affects your
livelihood?

He just said he had a rough morning but he's fine.

Well, the main thing is if he's doing this out of anger
and frustration to get back at you...

And if you give up out of anger and frustration, then
you lose out.

Somebody has to play the grownup.

And walking away would be the easiest thing to do.

You wanna make sure whatever you do, you won't

regret it.

She probably feels like she makes all the money and pays all the bills.

She feels out of control and then the kids lose.

Yeah.

Yeah.

Absolutely.

Did you go to that web site I sent you?

She's doing it because she's desperate.

And the best thing you can do is remain calm.

I know what that feels like, being the one to blame.

The one thing to remember is it takes two to tango.

I wouldn't even do all those things.

It's really your decision to do things the easy way or the hard way.

Yeah.

Right.

Unfortunately, yours has gotten way too far at this point.

Except you've been putting Band-Aids on it as an individual as opposed to doing it as a team.

They were sleeping in separate rooms.

For fifteen years they did this.

He works at night and she works during the day, so it's convenient.

They never saw each other.

Then they got divorced.

It's interesting what life gives you.

Yeah, if life gives you apples, you make applesauce.

And if it gives you lemons, you make lemonade.

She's going to use that whole thing to ruin your situation.

There was a case when the mother slapped the daughter.

The daughter smart-mouthed her.

Just when things were getting interesting, she got off at her stop. For a split second, I seriously considered following her, but...no.

# Voiceover Artist

Of all the species of cellophiles, the Voiceover Artist is probably the most narcissistic. More so than the Big Shot or the Social Butterfly!

It does not bask in the glory of its professional accomplishments or social connections.

While it makes a decent effort to maintain a pleasant appearance, it is not the source of its pride. Above all else, its voice gives this breed the self-esteem of cinematic proportions.

It usually demonstrates a respectable grasp of the English language. However, it is known to conjugate verbs incorrectly from time to time. The simple act of projecting its voice for everyone to hear provides a steady source of nourishment for this creature. Talking also polishes its scales to a glossy, multi-colored finish.

It will often prance about with its head held high, spreading its scales widely, while offering advice or "dropping knowledge" to the person on the other end. During this practice, sunlight bounces off its scales and the Voiceover Artist is in its element, displaying its wisdom for all to...enjoy?

I doubt that.

FaOA2g:   Donna?

I got the shit!

You gonna be there?

What?

You have to wait for things to get squared away?

What things to get squared away?

How is the number gone?

Did you have the number?

You don't have the number?

I was gonna get a ride to Brick Church anyway!

I don't believe you, Donna!

You know where your boy is?

So still come up there!

All right!

Bye!

--------------------

MaOA4k:   You took all my friends away form me!

You took Lana, Julie and Paul!

They don't talk to me anymore!

They knew me before they knew you!

OK!

OK!

OK!

I've known Lana since freshman year in college!

I've known Julie since the second grade!

I'm not trying to be!

I'm not trying to be!

I'm sorry!

I'm sorry!

I'm really glad you called!

No!

No!

No!

I completely understand!

Right. How about this? How many people did you know from

Orange County?

That's not my fault!

How many people do you know from Manhattan?

Again, that's not my fault!

Do you have any idea what me and Julie's relationship was?

You honestly said that you don't hang out with me anymore!

Apparently they do!

I'm not complaining about them!

You can keep them!

You honestly think it's like that?

You honestly think that they are more loyal to you than they are to me?

I know for a fact that they are!

No!

I'm asking you that you actually encouraged them to not talk to me?

I can't believe that!

When you came to Albany and you became friends with Brent!

How protective of him were you?

How many times did you tell me that he was **your** friend and not mine?

You actually did not sit on Julie's bed crying, telling her not to talk to me?

All right, I answered your questions, now you answer mine.

Did you sleep with that guy Tom?

You told me you did!

You only saw one guy for one night!

You actually did not cry on Julie's bed?

I know the truth here.

Are you sure?

Because I just want to make sure I got it straight.

And I'm going to give someone hell!

One of your friends.

It doesn't matter!

Have you slept with any other guys since we broke up?

How many?

I did.

A couple months ago.

Did I stutter?

Yeah, I'm here.

So, you didn't sleep with Tom but you did sleep with
    strangers?

Oh, so you lied!

I thought we had an agreement!

I answered two and you answered one and I answered
    that before the agreement!

This is such a retarded argument!

I **am** happy!

I am **so** happy right now!

No!

No!

No!

I don't want you to go!

Lindsay, I'm sorry!

Lindsay, I'm sorry!

I'm not half as mad at you as I am at them!

I said, "I'm not half as mad at you as I am at them!"

She wanted me to go with her dad!

You gotta understand that Julie has been my best friend since second grade! It feels like it is!

Because if you didn't know me, you wouldn't know her!

I'm sorry.

I'm sorry.

It feels like you took everything from me!

You took my friends—

I feel like you've taken everything that means anything to me!

I think you stripped me naked!

And I'm so mad at you for that!

Besides Stacy, Kara and the other girl—

I don't remember her name...Roxanne.

It feels like you've stolen everything from me!

You think I saw Barbara before you moved?

I'm really glad you called.

I know that I'll never see you again.

I'll say, 'Let's hang out.' But you'll never agree to it.

I think I'll say that and you'll say, 'That's so nice'—

Hello?

Hello?

--------------------

MaCM3j:   We're on the train, so we'll be there about 9:18.
          Go to the right side of the parking lot.
          Yeah.
          I don't want you sticking out.
          OK.

--------------------

FaCM6u:   What?
          Hello...
          Good.
          Who is this?
          No.
          Who is this?
          (laughs)
          Who is this?
          I'm on the train to...
          Who is this?
          I'm going to work.
          Who is this?
          Hello?
          Hello?

--------------------

MaCM8l:   First I have to find a cab.
          Right.
          OK.
          That sounds like a great idea!
          I'd like to do that.
          But let me check and see if I can get a cab.
          No, it's amusing.

Yeah.

We'll give you a call this weekend.

Yeah, but a real one is what we're looking for.

So, we'll talk to you.

OK.

Bye.

---------------------

FalE5c:   Hi, I'm on the train now.

It's not leaving till 8:44, so it won't be there till 9:07.

Brick Church.

Did you get e-mail?

Did you guys eat?

Go ahead and eat already, don't wait for me.

No, I have to work again tonight.

9:05, OK?

OK, bye.

---------------------

MaCM9m:   Hello?

Hello?

Someone call me?

I have my cell phone and it says I got a call.

Hello?

I'm still on the phone.

It says I got a call.

Hello?

Hello?

(looks at the phone) Shit!

---------------------

FaHR7y:   He rude!
          You see how he is?
          Mm-hmm!
          Yeah! But how you gonna do that?
          Oh my God!
          On the internet?
          Download on the internet.
          He got a loan from a loan shark!

She got off at East Orange.

---------------------

MaHR9x:   Yo!
          What's up, man?
          You get my message?
          You sound drunk as shit!
          Yo, listen. I got a business deal for you!
          I got a business deal for you!
          Call me when you get sober!
          Call me when you get sober!
          I'm serious!
          Bye.

---------------------

MaHR9h:   You ain't takin' care of those babies like you say you
          are!
          What's up with your girl?

What's up?
I'm still at work?
Yes I am!
Yeah!
I got a job!
I got a job!
I got a job!

He hung up and sighed heavily.

--------------------

MaBS3u:   I'm hooking up the satellite hook-up!
Yeah!
I met Chris Rock!
I met with Chris Rock!
Yeah, I'm meeting Chris Rock!
I'm in the loop, baby!
I told you!
I'm in the loop!
And when this goes down, I'm gonna hook up with
you guys because you're my A1 talent!
Yeah, you're my A1 talent!
Yeah!

He hung up and dialed.

What's up, baby?
Come on through!
You gotta come through!
I'm suited down!

I got the fedora and everything, baby!
Listen to this! Guess what?
I got three companies working for me!
(laughs)
Yeah, but don't tell nobody!
And—
Hello?
Tony?
Tony?

We entered a tunnel. He lost the signal. MaBS3u stared at its phone.

MaBS3u:     Aw, man. Shit! Come on, baby!

He dialed the number again.

Tony, real quick. Are we doing the Washington D.C.
    thing with Muhammad Ali?
Am I hanging the piece in the thing?
I knew all that!
I gotta get there early!
I gotta get in!
I gotta make preparations!
I got two pieces on Muhammad Ali!
They're nice!
So you gotta get me and Ron in, man!
You're gonna have lunch with us?
OK!
When do you go?
Around 1:30?
Something like that?

OK, man!
All right, man!
Come on through, man!
Yeah, man!
All right!

# Social Butterfly

This is the female counterpart of the BigShot.

Its goal is to make everyone aware that it is always on the go and has a very active social life. Not settling for mere acceptance, it needs to be loved and always wants to be the center of well-wishing attention.

The S.B. carries itself by fluttering its wings at a furious pace, much like a hummingbird. However, what is natural flight for the hummingbird, the exertions of the S.B. tend to look like a desperate plea for attention.

Its wings are kept strong and vibrant by a steady diet of compliments and preferential treatment from others. Unfortunately, the constant unfurling and flapping of these garish appendages inspire the exact opposite reaction on the train, for it is always the object of its fellow passengers' disdain.

To compensate for this, it is rarely without its supply of affection, which it sprays with its soft and sugary voice. However, the S.B. must take considerable care in the distribution of its fawning mist, for a more discerning ear might pick up just a hint of condescension.

FaMS1m:   I am on the train.
          I am on the train.
          I am on the train.
          I have an 11 o'clock appointment with my peer
              counselor.
          So, do you wanna do something after I'm done?
          OK.
              (laughs)
          OK.
          Just don't let me buy anything.
              (laughs)
          Only if it's under $10.
          Where are you?
          3rd and 38th?
          Well, I'm at 5th and 37th.
          You wanna meet at Megabyte?
          Megabyte?
          That's closer to Avenue of the Americas.
          That's closer to 6th.
          OK. I'll see you after I'm done with my peer
              counselor.
          OK.
          Bye.

--------------------

MaBS4s:   Hi, Ned. It's Peter.
          How you doin'?
          I'm going to have a meeting with some associates and
          I thought I'd bring you in.

You have a meeting?

We don't have a time set as of yet, but I thought I'd touch base with you and see if you're available.

So give me a call on my cell.

xxx-xxx-xxxx.

Maybe I should give you a call.

OK.

--------------------

FaCM7k:   She gave me some Vioxx for the pain.

She said they might need to give me injections for a couple of things and I don't want injections.

Well, you go rest.

Feel better.

Where are you meeting at?

That's a good idea.

Oh well.

I did not want to go today and I don't want to stay up.

Whoa!

That's what we did with them!

(laughs)

That's too bad for him!

You weren't even friends at that point.

He's staying with them because they're closer?

He's getting married in August.

Is that how you say his name?

I'm gonna be so upset if I get there and I get all this stuff in my face.

I'm gonna be so upset if I get there and I get all this stuff in my face.

I feel like I'm never gonna get there.

I mean, the last express train was like, 8:00 and I missed it.
Now I'm on the 9:00.
OK.

--------------------

MaMS1p:   What's her name?
          Bernice Stand?
          S...T...OK, Statton.
          Who's going to pick up these business cards?
          There's no way I'm going to be able to pick them up
             today!

He hung up and dialed a number.

          May I speak to Bernice Statton?
          Hi, Bernice?
          Hal Sick.
          Bill in LA wanted me to give you a call.
          I recently just sold my business and I'm looking to
             get into something else.
          I'm a CPA.
          Yes.
          Vice President of Finance at Macy's.
          I ran my own Foot Locker.
          Where do I live?
          I live in Bedminster but relocating to the
             Maplewood-Millburn area.
          Detail-oriented management.
          It's retail.
          Home furnishings.
          I ran it with my spouse.

We divorced, so...
You tell me.
Tuesday?
OK.
No problem.
Just like it sounds.
Uh, either one is fine.
xxx-xxx-xxxx.
That's my cell.
H [Sick 32 at hotmail dot com](). 
You got it.
OK, great.
OK.
Thanks, Bernice.
I appreciate your help.
Bye now.

and another number...

Hi, Beth. It's me.
Give me a holler. My cell phone is xxx-xxx-xxxx. OK, bye.

and another...

Hi, Rick. It's Hal Sick. I sent you my resume. I got your
email on Friday and I would love to talk to you. Give me
a holler on my cell,
OK? Thanks. Bye.

and another.

Hi, this is Hal Sick and I sent you my resume and I'm
    looking forward to talking to you. Again, it's Hal Sick and
I'm looking forward to getting a chance to talk.
Thanks.
Bye.

--------------------

The following conversation took place on a Wednesday morning.

FaCM6z:   Hi. It's Karen Reynolds.
          Is this Juliani or Rosetta?
          Hello?
          Hi.
          It's Karen Reynolds.
          How are you?
          OK.
          I got your message and it's OK to not come today.
          We're going to be away.
          We're going to Garden City and we won't be back till
              Sunday.
          I couldn't get a key under the mat because it was
              frozen, so you'll have to go in through the garage.
          There's a little box with a bunch of numbers on it.
          And you have to press xxxx and ENTER.
          xxxx.
          xxxx. And then you have to press ENTER.
          E-N-T-E-R and then the door will open.
          And the money will be on the table.
          OK?
          That's right, xxxx and then ENTER.
          We're actually going to be away, so you don't have to

call. OK?

Do you want my cell phone in case you have a problem?

OK, It's xxx-xxx-xxxx.

xxx-xxx-xxxx

OK?

Thanks, Juliani

Thank you.

Bye.

--------------------

MaBS4h:   I'm bouncing my check to the IRS, so I have to use the money to buy some stock.

I don't think I have a choice.

OK. So, the bank is Citibank.

The account number is xxxxxxxx.

The account number is xxxxxxxx.

Citibank, 3rd Avenue and 34th Street.

And the routing number is xxxxxxxxx.

And if you can confirm the transfer, that would be great!

OK.

Thanks again.

Bye.

--------------------

MaMS6x:   Hey!

How you doin?

I just called the wrong number and I got this stupid answering machine.

It was like, 'This is the office of Brent Spark.'

So, how you doin?

I was working late. Till 2:00 in the morning!
I got sixteen hours on the clock, baby!
So I gave him a discount of $40 an hour!
So I multiplied 40 times 16.
That should be $750!
I just wanna walk in the door clear!
So, how much is it?
Oh, it's $640?
OK. I'll do the 640 today and do the rest next week.
So, you got my card?
OK.
So, take that out and I'll see you in a little bit.
All right?
And I **did** medicate, OK?

--------------------

MaSB4c:    Hi!
           How'd it go?
           Everything was good.
           So, how's the little guy?
           Yeah! I'm in a great mood!
           It was great!
           He stayed for more drinks!
           I've never seen anything like that before!
           Yeah.
           Three Bloody Marys!
           Oh fantastic!
           Why don't you wait till I call?
           OK.
           See you then.

---------------------

FaMS0f:  Hey.

What you doin'?

I was callin' you.

No.

Is it working?

No.

No. I'm on the train.

I felt all right, but I needed some more
concentration as far as my classes are concerned.

I hope I can get enough credits to pass this class.

Then I'll have to take this other class.

I heard there was a fire.

I didn't see or smell anything.

I did hear the helicopters.

OK.

Bye.


---------------------

Mal03s:  What's up?

How you doin'?

OK.

OK.

What time you gonna be home, you think?

8:58 train. I'll be there at 9:30.

Have you been home yet?

Well, why don't you go home and start dinner?

All right.

I'll see you at 9:30.

OK.

Bye.

--------------------

MaCM5q:    Hey, man!
What's up?
You still in Massachusetts?
I'll call you back later.
What?
You're in Jersey?
No, you told me you were in Massachusetts!
I'm in the city today.
Yeah, I'll call you later.

He dialed again.

Hi. I got a call on my phone.
I got a call from you on my cell phone.
You called this number.
I got your number.
I was just calling to find out who it is.
It's OK.
I just got a call and I was just calling to find out who it is.
Hello?
Hello?

--------------------

MaMS7h:    I have the East Orange lease.
We need to get renters insurance.
We can do it one of two ways. We could--
We can't be doing money orders! That's ridiculous!

So we'll have to give the other money.

The landlord is not responsible for theft or damage.

They tried to stick me with a $1,000 fee and $100 for a
credit check.

So we're paying him $22,000 at the end of the year.

We have to mail it.

Yeah.

Are you going to leave cash or a check?

Are you sure this guy is in South Orange?

Water is included.

They have to have two smoke alarms and check for carbon
monoxide.

I'll just write the check.

All right.

I'll see you.

Bye.

--------------------

MaMS2w:    I'm on the 8:45.

It's a local, so I'd say about fifteen.

Well, you have to talk to Sara.

Yeah.

The tickets are $80.00 for the game.

It starts around 8:00 and it's for charity.

It's going to have newspaper and TV coverage
because it's a benefit for the

United Way, so a lot of people will be there and it's a
real bonding experience for father and son.

I only have two tickets.

I got them because somebody cancelled.

I don't know if I could get any more tickets.

It will be a chartered bus.

Yeah. I got it from a friend of mine.

It has a TV, satellite.

There's a bathroom on the bus.

Yeah. It's a real good bonding experience.

So, if I could get a ticket, would you and Timmy like to come?

(laughs)

You're such a good wife.

That's the right answer.

I had two tickets and I thought of you first.

OK. I can't promise anything.

If I could get another one it'll probably be a last minute thing. So all I can say is be ready, OK?

All right.

Take care.

He dialed again.

Hi. I'm on the train.

You happen to have two available?

Oh.

You only have one?

This was my stop.

# Foreign Copycat

This breed is just happy to be in America.

Its chameleon-like skin gives this creature the amazing ability to adapt to any environment. Because of this feature, the F.C. has very little difficulty emulating its American counterpart, right down to its sense of entitlement.

The F.C. feeds on a steady diet of assimilation, much to the chagrin of its countrymen overseas. Its patterns of speech, diet and customs indicative of its native land are quickly discarded for the American ideal.

Preening habits, standards of beauty, rudeness to others, (especially non-whites) are the means by which the F.C. strives to become more American. However, its ability to change its appearance has limits. While it can change the texture of its skin, the pigment remains constant, revealing its true origin.

Regardless of the length of time the F.C. spends in the States, it is also considered a minority, leaving it susceptible to the same treatment it exhibits toward other non-whites.

FaSB0o:   Doesn't anybody stay home on a school night for
          Pete's sake? OK, give me a call.

  She dialed again...

      Hi. It's me. I'm on the train. Give a call when you get
        this message, OK?
      Bye.

and again...

      Hi. It's me and I'm so blue. (laughs) Anyway, give me a call.

and yet again.

      Hi.
      I'm so hungry!
      No, I can't.
      I'm on the train.
      Did I talk to you yesterday?
      This is good.
      This is good.
      This is good.
      Guess what?
      I'm going on my date tomorrow!
      I've been emailing you all week!
      All right.
      I'm gonna be I M-ing you!
      No.
      No.
      I need someone to talk to while I'm on the train.
      OK.

Go back to your entertaining and—
Oh. Allen's there?
Oh, then by all means.
By all means.
OK. Talk to you later.
Bye.

--------------------

Fa7CMz:   Are you on break?
What did you get on your science test?
Was it below a ten?
Why did she have to sign it?
Because it was bad?
Was it good, like thirteen out of thirteen?
OK.
Bye.

--------------------

FaSB9t:   We might have to drive separately.
To sleep over.
I might have to clean out my office but there's a couch
   in there and Mike is in the living room.
Sure, just as long as I know.
I also asked Billy.
It's basically going to be an hour event.
Anyway, it's like December 25th.
Well, we're off on that day.
Is that OK?
Well, it's important.
Well, *I* think it's important!

It takes *that* long?

Wow!

Wow!

Wow!

So, October 16th is out?

OK.

That's a good sign.

That's OK. We'll just clean up.

We'll help you clean up before we leave.

OK?

OK?

OK?

All right.

I'll talk to you later.

OK.

I love you.

Bye.

--------------------

FaSB2r:    Hi, Jim. It's Justine.

Listen, my parents are in town and we're going to
meet Ralph for lunch.

Oh. You saw him?

Yeah.

Uh-huh.

Oh yeah.

OK.

OK.

I'm going home.

I ran over to Nancy's house.

He's a what?

A teller?

Why is he there at night?

Oh, that's very poor.

They can't afford to get married if that's what he's doing!

Oh my God!

Oh my God!

Oh...that's nice.

Oh.

Mm-hmm.

I might bring a nice salad, then.

The wedding is going to be there too?

At the church?

(sarcastically) I'm sure they're going to appreciate **that**!

Uh-huh.

Well, stick together.

So, is your mother around?

That's not what I thought I would ask.

Christy has her 50th wedding anniversary!

So, if she'd like to go...

You should go, too.

Why not?

It works out OK.

They have a special deal till October.

I'm not much of a driver myself.

OK.

I'll call you later.

OK. Bye.

--------------------

MaCM2p:   I'm on the train.

I'm in Hoboken now.

That's good.
Right.
Right.
Right.
That's good.
I think we're gonna move Kelly's stuff.
I'll talk to you tonight to see if it's a go.
Not that much.
Yeah.
Let me talk to her.
Yeah, just the big stuff.
Yeah, hopefully!
(laughs)
Yeah, they flare up every now and then.
I have no idea, dude.
I didn't call her.
Yep.
Yep.
Yep.
I know.
Oh yeah.
(laughs)
I'll email you.
I forgot to.
I'll email you.
Yeah, that's good to know.
That's all you need.
Yeah. I just have to figure out what I need.
Yeah.
Yeah.
What's he doing?
Sleeping?

(laughs loudly)

OK.

OK.

--------------------

MalO8x:    Hi.

This is Wilbur.

I'm just calling to wish you happy holidays, Merry Christmas, Happy Chanukah, Happy New Year and all that.

Give me a call.

Give me a call.

Give me a call.

Give me a call.

--------------------

MaCM7n:    Yo, Allen! What's up?

I was at the happy hour thing!

I'm on the train.

Happy hour was from 5 to 6.

I'm on my way to the barber.

You've gotta clean yourself up!

Yeah that's not a good credit card.

It's only got—

(laughs)

So, what's going on?

Yeah.

Yeah.

Yeah.

Yeah.

I'm on my way, yeah.
Yeah, that's my train.
(laughs)
Yeah.
Yeah
Yeah.
You know what?
You don't want to ride that.
It's not worth it.
I'm never gonna get home in time to go to the gym.
I'll get home around 5.
If I was living in Brooklyn and commuting to Manhattan--
I know it sounds crazy but, whatever.
About an hour and change.
The whole straphanger thing is not my thing.

We entered a tunnel.

T Mobile.
It works in tunnels.
Instead of going to the gym in my community because I
    don't want to look at old people.
I want to join a gym and have something to look at.
Not like people who are like, forty.
No, that's not for me.
(laughs)
Yeah.
Like computer geeks.
Yeah. They always have to update the website.
No. I'm going to pick up the girls.
But it's nice to know I have the option.
Yeah.

Right.

Hmmm.

So, it's like, collecting credit card numbers.

Right.

Orange is next.

Yeah.

OK.

Mmm-hmm.

Right.

Right.

Right.

"Dot org" and all that.

It's a non-profit organization?

Right.

Yeah.

Right.

OK. I'll talk to you.

He dialed another number.

Hi.

I'm in Orange.

I just wanted to tell you that.

This crowd was—

What are you guys doing?

All right. I'll be in Orange in fifteen minutes.

"You are the rudest person I have ever seen on the train! You were loud and rude! You owe everyone in this train car an apology! Stop it!"

-- Passenger to a cellophile

The cellophile was too stunned to reply.

# Soundbites

The following is a collection of small bits of conversations I heard while walking about in train stations, on the streets and station platforms. Fill in your own story.

FaVA8f:   And then at one point, they were saying, 'You're a fag!' 'No! You are!'
'No! You're a fag!' 'No! You're a fucking fag!' Then I said, 'No one's a fucking fag! Just settle it!'

FaBS3m:   I don't care what nobody say about my life, 'cause being thirty don't mean shit!
I know I'm thirty but I look young!
I got a good body and I'm in the city!
And that's what you gotta do!

FaMS0h:   You are like a computer. We are like computers. And this project is like...like...the software. And when we use our hardware to work out the problems, there's nothing we can't do!

MaHR1w:   Get the fuck outta here!

FaSB7v:   What are you doing up there?
I'm on the train. I'll be there about 7:30

MaMS9p:   Yeah. I wanna do a new website and shit!

FaIE5m:   I haven't looked at it. Some of the stuff is ten years old, all right?

MaBS2s:  That's why I keep telling you to join! They're gonna treat you the same way they treat me...

MaCM8w:  I think it's bullshit but—
(laughs)
On what?
(laughs)
OK, I'll talk to you later.

FaVA3k:  Hi, Matthew. What's up?
What's **that** all about?
(laughs)
Piano wire?

FaOA4n:  You don't have a choice. You have a very stupid customer!
You don't have a choice, Andrew!
That's not possible.
Right.
Right.
Mm-hmm...

FaOA5h:  Is Reggie or Janice available or are they in meetings?
Yes.
Beg your pardon?
(frustrated sigh) 2:00 is fine.

FaOA6f:  I didn't realize I had to call you every hour!
Yes, Mother!
OK! Good-bye!

FaIE8b:    I fuckin' hate this city!

MaSB7r:    I met a woman who's all about it!
           I met a woman who's all about it!

FaOA0t:    We didn't get it!
           The insurance people didn't get it!
           Ken didn't send it to them!
           No!
           Mommy! Did you hear anything I said? The insurance
               people didn't get it!

MaSB8z:    It's OK.
           I think some of it is touching and some of it is odd.
           It's odd.
           It's odd.
           Why don't we get together next week
               and...umm...umm...

FaOA3o:    Go to your room, Shawn!
           I don't care!
           I just told you!
           Go to your fuckin' room!


MaOA2b:    He has access to the house because I left the other
               door unlocked!

MaVA4y:    There are two things that land you in trouble...your
               attitude and your mouth!

MalE4v:    Yeah, well, things happen for a reason.
           Yeah.
           Yeah.
           Strong woman.

FaOA0k:    Mom!
           I checked the email!
           I checked the fax!
           What are you saying?
           Listen before you freak out!
           If I had checked it, I would have known!
           Seriously!

MaCH6v:    I'm Puerto Rican and Black but I got, like a tan-like
           skin. I'm not dark as hell but I'm like, tan-skinned.

MalO5s:    Yeah.
           I'm walking down the street.
           (sirens wail)
           Yeah. Typical city background noise.
           It's amazing!
           There's so many people! And buildings! And cars!


FaCH9n:    ...and I gotta get food today, so I can't help you.

FaMS0j:    I feel like shit, but I'm coming around!

FaMS7p:    Not another soul will take advantage of me...ever!

MaVA9e:    I had to pay on Father's Day, so don't give me that
           shit!

MaCH0z:   If I send a text to one bitch, saying, "I miss you", all
          the other ones will get it!

FaOA3q:   Are you lying to me right now?

# Dear New Jersey Transit

Please stop blowing your horns/whistles and ringing your bells while approaching/leaving the stations. Don't tell us that these noisy intrusions are for our safety. Announcements are always made over the P.A. system to notify customers when a train is arriving, so we're always aware of incoming traffic. You are only contributing to the noise pollution in our communities.

It is especially annoying when you feel the need to make noise as your express trains zip past our stations. No one is on the platform, so there is no need to sound a warning.

The trains in New York don't make so much noise.

FaSB6b:     I don't know if I want to go to the mall.
            Because tomorrow is like, Saturday, so it might not be
                good.
            So, maybe we could look into other options or
                whatever.


The train entered a tunnel, so the cellophile was silent for a few
moments.

            I'll call you when I like, get off the train or whatever.
            It might work out better because it's not going to be
                like, busy.
            That might be like, better.
            That sounds like, fun.
            OK.
            So, I'll like, call you around like, 12:30.
            OK.
            I can't wait!


                        --------------------


FaSB1v:     Hello.
            Hi, Jane. How are you?
            Is that good?
            Uh-huh.
            Mm-hmm.
            That's right.
            We're gonna have to go back in a few days.
            Monday is not good and uh...
            Um, Tuesday?
        Wednesday looks good.
        The 8th and I'm leaning towards Thursday.

Friday looks clear.

Great.

Keep in mind that I'll be looking into other possibilities,
OK?

I'll put down lunch but—

Yeah.

OK.

So, I'll talk to you soon.

OK, bye.

--------------------

FaSB3c:   (laughs)

I don't think you guys are supposed to be there.

It's a shower.

A baby shower.

I'm sorry.

They're so modern!

Are you going?

I'm checking my calendar.

The week before Thanksgiving, which is on a
Friday.

OK.

Bye.

--------------------

MaCM4r:   I would take Matty out of daycare.

And I would get one of those hotels?

What do you call them?

'Apartments to lease', yeah.

I would wind up selling the Cadillac.

No more pimpmobile.

We feel good about selling because the house across the
street sold for 290K.

We would be happy with 270.

We don't have a driveway but our property is bigger.

The company was acquired by McDonald's in 1999.

I was interviewed by two people.

Then three people.

I get a car, internet access. They pay for two meals when
I'm on the road.

The typical employees are teenagers and elderly.

The main issues are cash issues, theft, robberies.

I didn't ask that question but they do a certain amount of
transactions per hour.

They don't disclose financial information.


A man across from me found it difficult to read with the
cellophile talking so loudly. After a futile attempt to get the
cellophile's attention by coughing and clearing his throat loudly,
he threw his head back and sighed very loudly. The cellophile
continued.


Yeah.

This is one of them.

Oh.

(scoffs loudly)

Great.

Yeah.

So you have some options.

Yeah.

However, they're not giving you a chance right now.

Uh, yes they do, but if you have a complaint about Bill to

James, it would because he likes to gossip.

If he likes a person, he goes to bat for them.

I think James doesn't like to rock the boat.

He's good at playing both sides.

I don't think he tries to form an opinion about
someone but he does.

Like, we had a thing in Short Hills and things went awry
and he said, 'I didn't plan it that way.'

Hello?

Hello?

I'm here.

I think it's going to come down to Becky not giving
you a fair chance.

If you get promoted, you'll be fighting her tooth and
nail all the way.

And you'll back down.

And you have to let her know she needs to inform
you about things.

Speaking of divas, my girl Mariah Carey has a new album.

I have to pick that up.

She's by far my favorite.

As far as all the divas.

Give it some time. It'll grow on you.

Give it some time. It'll grow on you.

I have our late people come in at 12:00.

Remember, we work seven and a half hour days.

I guess what I should do is do a search in-service.

That's my only recourse.

I have no idea.

I don't know.

I guess it's part of the reason I feel guilty.

I do understand why people feel the way they do, working
in our store.

Yeah.

I'm about to go into a tunnel, so I'm going to lose you.

OK.

So, I'll talk to you soon.

OK.

# Mover/Shaker

Though it is one of the smallest of cellophiles, its call tends to lead the listener to believe it is larger than it is. This cousin to the Big Shot wants everyone to know that it is in the process of some epic business plan, or attending some big social event.

The Mover/Shaker voices opinions about any given subject to demonstrate its (imaginary) extensive knowledge. It lives on a steady diet of taking pride in telling everyone within earshot how much things cost, as if to announce the fact that money is no object.

This species lacks the eye-catching plumage of the Big Shot or the Social Butterfly, for its dull and split hairs are usually made of estimates, lengths of time, amounts of various materials, deadlines, prices, labor costs, etc. But that does not deter it from leaving the impression that it is making big plans and getting things done. In reality however, most of these projects only amount to small tasks, such as purchasing a new toilet for its burrow, or planning a birthday party for its offspring.

MaCM6m:   Hello, Jennifer?

It's Patrick Allston.

How are you?

I'm just heading out to—

No I have not.

Mmm-hmm.

Mmm-hmm.

Right.

Right.

I hear you.

Well, I've been meaning to talk to her after the meeting, but I was so busy and I would forget.

That's why I thought I'd reach out to tell her my concerns.

Have I talked to whom?

No, not recently.

Mmm.

Well, listen. Let him know that I called and that I'll reach out to him. OK?

And how are you?

And the kids?

Mmm-hmm.

I'm sure she's not.

That's obvious.

That's obvious.

Mmm-hmm.

Mmm-hmm.

Mmm-hmm.

Mmm-hmm.

Mmm-hmm.

Mmm-hmm.

Mmm-hmm.

Mmm-hmm.

Mmm-hmm.

Do you have the opportunity to talk to anyone?

Are you comfortable handling it by yourself?

I can't hear you.

I got that.

Two weeks of training and then you're off.

All right then.

I'll talk to him.

--------------------

MalE9u:  Hey.

Excuse me?

Wow!

Yeah.

Probably, yeah.

Yeah.

Yeah.

Yeah.

I'll find something.

Yeah.

All right.

OK.

OK.

Yeah.

OK.

Call him up.

--------------------

FalE4j:    Hey!

What's up?

How you doin'?

How was Christmas?

How was Christmas?

How was Christmas?

What did you get for Christmas?

What did you get for Christmas?

What did you get for Christmas?

What did you get for Christmas?

You got a doll?

Did you see her?

What did she say when you seen her?

What did she say when you seen her?

What did she say when you seen her?

So, did Jim come over?

Did Jim come over?

Did Jim come over?

Oh, he didn't come?

What happened?

You didn't call him?

Oh, he had to work?

Javion?

Javion?

Javion?

What kind of name is that?

Well..."Javion". It's different.

I'm on the train.

What?

What?

Y'all comin' to the house?

Y'all comin' to the house?

Huh?

You get out what time?

12:00.

So you might be gettin' out there when I get out there.

If you get out early, call me.

OK.

Bye.

--------------------

FaFC5b:   Right.

Yes.

Mm-hmm.

Right.

Yes.

Mm-hmm.

Right.

Yes.

Mm-hmm.

No.

He wasn't down the store.

He was saying this morning.

He said get out there.

They were stepping on the pavement last night.

Mm-hmm.

Him said he didn't want to go to some other place.

Right.

Uh-huh.

Right.

Yes.

Mm-hmm.

Right.

Yes.

Mm-hmm.

He don't want to do it.

Yes.

Mm-hmm.

Yes.

Mm-hmm.

Yep.

Mm-hmm.

Mm-hmm.

Mm-hmm.

She wants you to take care of her personal business.

Mm-hmm.

Yep.

Mm-hmm.

Yep.

She's generally shy.

No.

Yes.

Oh, yes.

His mother is going to Virginia because there is another daughter.

Yes.

She was good.

Linda is wearing white.

(laughs)

She's sexy looks.

I guess it's the only thing in white she find.

(laughs)

It's sexy looking.

She have to try it.

She have to try it.

Yes.
And she's so well behaved.
It's last month.
He was behaving.
Bye.

--------------------

MaMS3q:     I understand why the stuff wasn't delivered yet.
            Do you have any idea when they'll get there?
            Early this afternoon?

He hung up and dialed.

Yeah, John.
Lenny had trouble with his truck so he couldn't
    deliver the stuff.
He said he could deliver it early this afternoon.
He didn't say. He—
I'm sorry?
I'm sorry?
He didn't say. He just said early this afternoon.
You wanna check this afternoon?
Are you working tomorrow?
OK.
You can check around 2:00.
If not, we'll see Monday.
OK.
Thank you.

--------------------

MaFC9z:    Hey.

Hmm.

Mm-hmm

How'd it go?

Mm-hmm

Everything OK?

Mm-hmm.

Huh?

Huh?

What did you do?

What?

(foreign language)

Huh?

(foreign language)

Huh?

(more foreign language)

Huh?

(still more foreign language)

A few English words slipped out during this string of Russian-sounding words, like "New York", "you know", "disgusting" and "uh-huh" but I didn't need a translator to determine that he was talking about the same thing his English-speaking counterparts talk about; absolutely nothing.

--------------------

A Foreign Copycat was talking very loudly in the next row. He must have considered himself quite a comedian because he laughed a lot while he talked.

He talked for some time. Some of the other passengers start cracking jokes about him. I couldn't hear what they were saying over the cellophile's cackling, but I did catch a few phrases like '...he thinks...' '...first time on a cell phone.', '...only one on the train...' followed by laughter. One of the passengers got off at an employee stop. Before departing, he glanced at the cellophile, shook his head slowly and laughed.

Several minutes later, a conductor entered the car. He approached the cellophile and motioned for him to keep it down. The cellophile continued to talk for a few minutes before finally signing off.

MaFC4d:   I'm supposed to pick up my car on Friday.
          $547.00.
          $531.80.
          How much?
          How much I pay?
          You take cash?
          Credit card?
          Can you take a check?
          You no take a check?
          Case number 67476.
          I go to pick up my car.
          67476.
          What?
          91 Chevy Nova.

My name is—
What?
What address?
What floor?
What floor?
First floor?
Second floor?
All right.

--------------------

MaFC6t:  What's a pretty lady like you doing out so late?
Then we laughed.
He said, "Was that a joke?"
I said "Yeah."
(foreign language)
I'll come there first.
Right now.
Someone is supposed to meet me with a truck.
Yeah.
You know what I mean?
(more foreign language)
Yeah.
Yeah
Because I know what I'm getting.
(laughs)
Right. Right.
I know, I know.
(more foreign language, followed by hearty laughter)
If I really want to go...
(more foreign language)
Yeah, man.

Right.
Right.
Right.
Right.
Right.
Yeah.
Yeah.
Yeah.
Yeah.
Yeah.
Yeah.
Nah. Nah. You know.
(more foreign language)

He got off the train.

# Idle Chatter

Probably the most pathetic of all cellophiles, the Idle Chatter has does not have any distinguishing plumage or fur, but a translucent outer shell, which only serves the purpose of protecting its innards from the elements. Unfortunately, this allows a view of said innards and probably, its equally unattractive soul.

Its diet consists of droning on and on in a rather irritating voice about the events of its day - which are always uneventful - and its current state of being, which is usually tired or hungry.

It might be coincidental, but the Idle Chatter's call is usually interrupted by a dropped signal. My guess would be that the person on the other end pretends to lose the call, saving him/herself from this rather boring species.

# Idol Chatter

This common breed exhibits a rather disturbing predilection for worshipping the person on the other end, while at the same time, finding a way to praise itself.

Its diet consists of sweet compliments and embarrassment-inducing flattery. Upon closer observation, I began to wonder at first, if this breed's profusion of accolades denotes a desperate need to be liked or something far more sinister. Unfortunately, the I.C. does not appear to have the intellectual wherewithal to pull off condescension.

While some of the Idol Chatter's characteristics resemble those of the Social Butterfly, its external features serve the same organ-protective function as its homonymic sister species and not meant to be attractive.

These two species often populate social media sites, where their dietary needs are often met more efficiently by a steady flow of likes and positive comments.

FaCM8s:   Yeah.
          No.
          No.
          Not this minute.
          She knows what to do.
          No.
          That's not what she's saying.
          Hello?
          Hello?
          Yeah?
          Hello?
          Hello?


-------------------


FaSB7q:   Hello!
          Hi!
          How are you?
          I'm fine!
          What are you up to?
          Well, we're on our way to the city!
          Yeah!
          You wanna say hi?
          Ok.
          Well why don't you bring them over?
          Yeah! It'll be great!
          Ok!
          Great!
          Ok!
          We'll see you soon!
          Ok!
          Bye!

----------------------

FaCM2f:   Hello?
          Hello?
          Who is this?
          Huh?
          Huh?
          Huh?
          I can't hear a word you saying.
          Huh?
          You sick?
          Huh?
          What made you sick?
          Huh?
          My train is gonna stop at Mountain.
          Huh? Mother layin' down?
          Sitting up?
          You can't make it?
          All right.

----------------------

FaIE3w:   Hello.
          Alice?
          You there?
          Hello?
          Hello?
          I must be in a dead zone.
          Hi, Alice?
          It's Karen.
          Are you there?
          Oh.

You are.

Um, I'm on the train.

I was supposed to go with my sister-in-law but she
    canceled.

Hello?

Hello?

--------------------

FalE8k:    Hi, Danny.

We just pulled out of the station.

Uh-huh.

Can you hear me?

You're dropping out.

I can't hear you very well.

Uh-huh.

OK.

OK.

OK.

I love you, too.

--------------------

FaCM5n:    What?

What?

What?

What?

What?

What's the number?

It's an hour and a half! It sucks!

But it's hard though because there's a train that goes
    straight from Penn Station.

What?

What?

Probably will.

What?

Not on purpose!

You hit your head against the wall?

Yeah, you would!

(giggles)

What?

Yeah, as long as you don't mess around with it.

No.

I'm not talking about that!

You're sick!

Yeah!

Yeah but you're making me sick!

What?

Something I did?

How's that?

(laughs)

What?

What?

That's when I came in.

That's when I came in.

No.

I just don't want you waiting that long.

When I figured you didn't see me you would keep walking.

Bye.

--------------------

FalE1d:    Hi, Ken, it's Mommy.

I was wondering if you were coming home for

Thanksgiving since you have three days off?

Oh.

So you won't be able to come?

You didn't—

Oh, you did go?

What happened?

Did you have to say anything?

Did they ask you anything?

Look, I can't understand you.

I'll have to call you back.

This is a bad connection.

--------------------

MalEOw:   Hey. How'd it go?

How'd it go?

Can you hear me?

I'll call you back in—

Hello?

Hello?

Hi.

I'm sorry. I'm on my way out of the city.

I'm on the train out of the city.

Call me back in fifteen minutes.

OK.

--------------------

FaSB6k:   Hello.

This is Melissa.

How are you?

I'm fine.

Good.

OK.

Fine.

I'm sorry.

I'm on the train and I didn't hear you. Could you repeat
   that?

Is it all right for you to hold them?

I'm gonna need the schedule.

I won't be in town.

But we'll call you when it gets close to the date.

I lost you.

I can't hear you.

I'll have to call you back.

--------------------

FaSB8v:     Hi, Nancy!

            Happy New Years!

            Yeah, I'm just really, really tired.

            Listen, I was thinking we could get together on
               Monday.

            Is that good for you?

            Oh, is that Martin Luther King's Day?

            Already?

            Oh my God!

            Well, how about Tuesday?

            Maybe we could—

            (stares at the phone)

            Oh, I lost her.

--------------------

FaOA4q:   What?
          Spell that!
          I can't understand what you're saying!
          What?
          "F" as in what?
          Don't scream!
          Don't scream!
          That's why I can't understand you!
          OK.
          Tell him I'm on the train!
          I'm in Newark!

She hung up quickly with a forceful button press.

--------------------

A female Hero approached a cellophile and asked her to lower her voice.

FaOA2h:   I lowered my voice!

The Hero returned to her seat.

FaOA2h:   There was no reason to even touch me!
          (returns to its call)
          I'm so pissed!
          This woman just told me to lower my voice!

Despite being pissed, she behaved for the rest of the trip.

--------------------

FalO0s:    Hi.

I'm on my way home.

I'm on the train.

I started my new job on Monday.

OK.

I started my new job.

It involves more travel than agreed upon.

I'm going to start looking for a new job.

All right.

I'll call you back.

Where are you?

When I find out what my schedule is, I'll call you.

What time are you going to be there?

Till five?

I'll definitely call you before then.

OK.

Bye.

She dialed again.

Hi, Mr. Barnes?

This is Carol Barker.

I got your message.

Sorry I couldn't get back to you.

I was busy all day till 5:00, but by then it was too late.

I was in Soho and I couldn't call. I would really like to meet
    with you.

Maybe during my lunch.

Saks Fifth Avenue at the Bobbie Brown corner.

xxx-xxx-xxxx.

She hung up and dialed again.

Hi, Becky?

It's Carol Barker!

How are you?

How's the baby?

Congratulations!

You know, I'm still waiting for that check.

I signed the agreement.

Could you check to see if it's there?

I know he said it is, but could you check to make sure it's there?

Thanks.

I signed it back in November.

I'd hate to annoy him with this, but I am in such need for money.

I'm on my way to work.

I work at Saks Fifth Avenue in New York City and I don't have my schedule for next week but I will have it by 5:00.

I'm looking at an hour and forty minutes to get to work.

I have to take two trains and the bus and it's such a big mess.

I don't know if he'll do it.

I know that he's OK with that.

Maybe he can waive the fees for this settlement and move them over to the new settlement.

I figured since they were so close together he could move the fees.

He really is a good guy.

And I'm so desperate for money.

Maybe he will do it and maybe he won't. Then what am I gonna do?

OK?

So, how's the baby?

Did he survive OK?

Oh, it was nice out today.

You want to be out.

Oh, OK.

Oh, OK.

Oh, OK.

Do you have a place downstairs for me?

Yeah, well, I put on eleven pounds.

You're telling me 'good'?

(laughs)

OK.

Well, congratulations, new mommy!

I'll talk to you again!

Bye!

# OverActor

This species has very thin, sensitive skin, which is covered with scraggy strands of hair, the results of a rich diet of melodrama. When agitated, the skin forms unsightly goose bumps, causing the hairs to stand on end, giving it the appearance of a human male with sparsely planted hair plugs.

It emits a shrill cacophony of interjections and complaints about whatever situation it is currently facing, much to the ire of those around it.

MaMS3n:     OK.

Well, I'm not in my office today but I will be in tomorrow morning. So we can talk then, OK?

He dialed again...

Hello?
Yep.
16 ½ what?
Right. 140 to 141.
OK.
OK.
Nah.
That's all.
See you later.

and again...

Hey, Jake. How are you?
I'm on the train to New York. How are you?
I'm actually meeting Mr. Russo.
I think they're moving close.
I think they're moving close.
Maybe I'll get more out of him today.
It's looking good.
Did you put it back at 16, 16 and a half?
I should know more tomorrow.
The institution is putting a big chunk of money.
We'll know tomorrow.
Yeah, it looks good, but things need to be perfect.
There are no concerns, OK?

All right.

I'll call you tomorrow.

and  again.

Hello?

Hi. How are you?

Not that I know of.

Not that I know of.

I'm on the train heading to the city at this moment.

We're busy.

We're in planning.

I know he's anxious to get back.

He's probably leaving in two days.

No! It's not an emergency and it's not any trouble!

We'll probably come in at 2 or 3.

I'm in a tunnel, so if I lose you, I'll call you back.

Are you there?

He closed his phone slowly.

Funny, we were nowhere near a tunnel.

--------------------

MaOAOy:    I left Lance.

He fuckin' stuck me!

I need the shit!

We gotta have a talk.

Uh...I don't need anybody to make money!

And I don't think it's fair to put any additional
pressure on me!

I emailed Tom.

I told him that Friday would be better.

Um…and my cousin combined have forty years of retail footwear.

That's true.

All right.

You'll forward me some info?

All right.

--------------------

FaCM7s: We were originally forecasted to do 65 books, but we don't have 65 books.

We just have the 32 and the ones on the wall, whatever that adds up to. 52?

OK. Do we have the money guide, too?

OK.

Very good.

I'll talk to you later.

Bye.

--------------------

MaMS2x: Why not?

OK, put him on.

Hi, James.

The thermostat is for the regulator.

You just have to run cables.

Do the wires run or do we have bad connecting?

Right.

So, does the wire run or it doesn't run?

What about the I.S.O. 4232?

That's great!

We were looking for a U-shaped device.

It's a detecting.

Well, it's a $10 piece of equipment.

Yeah, it looks like a matchbook with little contacts.

Now, the only thing I want to know is if he's got any steam
left in him is to run the MBF.

Yeah, well, it's out and Jimmy felt if you could do both...

It's all on an adjacent wall.

Why don't you do with the MBF, which is the critical one,
then we'll get Mike and read it?

All right.

Thanks, James.

Oh my God! I didn't think you'd be going at it all day for
God's sake!

Make sure you put the johnson pins and the leak detector.

Oh. We're not using the john—

So we have to do the cracked unit?

Oh my God.

So, on Monday we'll do the 650 and we'll do the rest
ourselves.

OK.

Have a good weekend.

--------------------

FaMS7x:   The first one is listed at $30.

That one is good.

The next one is at $35.

That never should have been ordered.

The second book was never ordered.

It was sent to someone's daughter and we talked to
the daughter and she never got the two books.

So we should be credited $35.

And the $5.

And the book that we ordered online, we should be credited.

And we should have four bonus books because we get four books for every one-hundred books and we only got one.

And to be honest, the only reason I ordered that many is because they were half price.

Yeah, but you still owe us money.

(laughs)

Well, I only did it because they were half price.

Yeah.

OK.

I'll talk to you before Passover.

You know what I'm going to make?

Matzo lasagna.

Have you ever heard of it?

Well, first you need a deep baking pan.

I use a glass pan.

Then, I put in one layer of matzo, one layer of tomato sauce, one layer of cottage cheese.

I can only do American cheese.

Add ¼ cup of water.

It's delicious.

It's soft when it's finished, so you can cut it in certain pieces.

And I have it for lunch and for the kids and visitors.

OK.

Very good.

Bye.

She dialed again...

Hi.
This is Sally Douglas.
I got a call from Alice. Is she in?
I don't know what it's about.
I was there on time!
I was there on time!
I don't care!
I was there on time!
It doesn't matter before eleven!
xxx-xxx-xxxx!
As I said, you do whatever is best for you!
But I have to say the only reason I bought that many is
    because it was half price!
I'm just being honest!
OK!
Bye!

and again.

Hi, Patsy.
It's Sally Douglas.
You called and spoke about the Montclair, right?
(sighs loudly)
I have to say that it's very difficult to do that!
I'm not saying that we don't do it, but I only give $100!
Yeah.
I give to the local EMS workers because they help us! You
    know what I mean?
That's the way I would ask.
I don't think so, but I'll ask.

Let me ask you a question.

How many people can I bring?

No more than that?

OK.

OK.

Bye.

--------------------

MaBS4w:  David, my man!

How are you?

What are you up to for lunch today?

It's **me**!

That's all right.

Yeah. Because I'm meeting a couple of people at
    Morgan-Stanley.

And we'll probably do something after.

Yeah, so if you wanna join us...

OK.

Bye.

He dialed.

Yes, may I speak to Ken, please?

Buenos dias, my man!

Yeah!

That guy had some interesting ideas. So maybe we
    could talk to Lenny.

This guy is **so** Morgan-Stanley!

It's scary!

He's got some really scary stuff!

He's a retail broker. So I wanna put you guys
    together.
OK.
Hold on. We're going through a tunnel.
You there?
What's my phone?
Motorola.
Yeah, it's the silver one.
Yeah. I'm really happy with this phone.
He's totally hardcore.
He went to school for it.
I had this idea and I brought it to Morgan-Stanley.
His best friend is one of the top producers.
Well, not the top, but one of them. But I want to bring him
    and his buddy in and give them their own branch.
Could you put together a deal for $350 million?
Now's the time to strike because everyone else is staying
    away from it.

He proceeded to the vestibule and out of earshot.

After listening to cellophiles and observing other passengers for so long, I developed an intense dislike for everyone. My thoughts became very dark and hateful. I needed a break, so I donned my headphones and busied myself with...

# A Few Notes on Commuter Culture

For those who do not ride the train on a regular basis:

When you board the train, it is important for you to remember that you are a guest. Show consideration for those who live here (commuters).

If you see someone in a two-seater with a bag on the seat next to him/her, it is an unspoken petition for privacy and personal space. Just imagine a sign over this person's head that reads, **"I DO NOT WANT MY SPACE INVADED. PLEASE FIND SOMEWHERE ELSE TO SIT."** However, if the need to sit down overrides your manners, **ASK THE COMMUTER POLITELY** if you could sit. He/She will gladly move the bag, but be warned. Although you will be forgiven--and even tolerated as this person holds up his/her end of a conversation you might initiate--the sooner you leave, the better. If you start a conversation and the person just smiles, back off. Stop talking. You are only being annoying.

Remember to **ASK POLITELY** for permission to sit. Don't just hover over the seat and assume the bag will be moved for you. He/She might do it just because you are standing there, but this will only prove that this individual is more highly evolved than you are. It is always better to **ASK POLITELY**. For those of you who lack this basic bit of home training because the only indication your parents are human is the fact that they walk on two legs, here is a phrase you could use:

"Excuse me, may I sit here?"

It's as simple as that. No speeches. No rudeness. Just plain old decent behavior. However, I must remind you that you really should find somewhere else to sit.

When you are at the train station and need a place to sit, look for the waiting room. Every station has one with plenty of seats for you and even your luggage. **DO NOT SIT ON THE STAIRS!** Stairs are used to navigate the floors, up or down. Much like the seats you would find at fast-food restaurants, stairs are not designed for comfort. Besides, you look like an absolute moron sitting there while hundreds of commuters are trying to walk around you! This is one of those moments when many people will simultaneously wish you a slow and painful death just before the happiest moment of your pathetic life is about to occur. And with so many minds working in agreement, it just might happen.

To the conductors:

**Open all of the cars.** It will not kill you to walk a few extra feet to collect tickets. Seriously, some of you could use the exercise. I only mention this out of concern for your health.

**Close the doors.** We **do not** enjoy the sound of scraping metal while the train is in motion. Also, the smell of your train's emissions is not at all pleasant. It spoils the meal for those who wish to eat on the train.

**Kindly clip the tickets toward the center of the aisle.** Ticket clippings do nothing to compliment our hair or clothing.

If the train is delayed, there is no need to make the same announcement every two minutes. You are not reporting breaking news to anyone just joining us. While we are sitting in the middle of a field on the outskirts of metropolis, no one else has boarded the train since the last announcement. Make them only when the status of our situation has changed. We know that "when we get a more favorable signal", we will proceed to the next stop. Hearing the same announcement over and over is annoying.

Please do not use the intercom to tell passengers to use the middle seats. No one likes to use them. Those "three-seaters" only have enough room for two, and the "two-seaters" can only accommodate one. The extra "seat" is for our bags. We would use the overhead luggage racks, but you guys don't keep them clean.

Train station personnel:

Customers need to be informed when a track is closed. Please place a sign at **EVERY** entrance so that people will not miss their train. Some of us like our careers and do not wish to be late for work.

Ticket window attendants:

When someone says "Good morning", reciprocate. We understand; you are miserable and will go out of your way to make life difficult for others. Try being nice to people. We are not asking you to share your views on current events (uninterested) or whip out photos of your children (inappropriate) or render service with a flashy smile and a song on your lips (creepy). We just want the first encounter with someone outside our homes to be a pleasant one. If this concept is beyond your reach, ponder this; how would you want your mom to be treated? Act accordingly.

Please arrange your paperwork and/or count your cash drawer **AFTER** you have served all customers. Please don't make us wait for you to get yourself together. It is not our fault you lack vital organizational skills to do your job efficiently. Remember, it does not take a quantum physicist to distribute train tickets. So, relieve yourself of the delusion that you possess any amount of power or prestige in your chosen profession. Think of these three words; Ticket Vending Machine.

Passengers:

On behalf of passengers sitting in front of you, please keep your feet off the seats! We can feel them. It is annoying. It borders on sexual assault when you are trying to dig your feet into our butts!

Do not cross your legs. We do not wish to spend our commute with your knee pressed against our backs. If you're going to provide such a lousy massage, the least you could do is treat us to a happy ending.

It is rude to allow your bag to knock against every seat as you walk down the aisle.

Do not use the seats to spread out your breakfast/lunch/dinner. Sure, it's OK to eat on the train—though NJ Transit may beg to differ—but you don't have to take up so much space in the process. Those seats are for people and their bags. Consider this; you are eating off a surface that has cradled millions of strangers' rears for several decades. This fact carries a considerable amount of weight during the spring and summer months. But if you're OK with having essence of swamp-ass with your meal, bon appetite!

Real men plant their feet on the floor. Guys, you look like high school girls with your feet on the seats. Cut that crap out! High school girls, you look like hookers in training with your legs in the air. Put them down!

Real ladies cross their ankles, not their legs.

If you board the train and spot a familiar face, do not stand in the aisle and chat away. Chances are someone is behind you. Be aware of your surroundings.

In the event of a delay, do not pout. Read a newspaper. Put on your headphones. Text someone you love. You are still alive. You are healthy. You have a job.

If you eat on the train, chew with your mouth closed. No one wants to hear the impact of teeth colliding, tongues smacking or saliva preparing your food for optimum swallowing.
Sometimes, the train is not as packed as you think. You just have to be willing to walk a few feet to find a seat.

What...are they saving seats for a rainy day?

-- Passenger, after finding one of the cars closed

After a month-long stretch of rehabilitation, I was ready to get back to observing life forms on the train.

MaBS5z:   Hey!

How you doin', kid?

Yeah.

I'm on the train.

How far out are you?

How far away are you?

Can you hear me?

He dialed again...

Hey, man!

I'm feeling good, man!

I wanna get that money!

I want ten loans processed!

I'm serious!

I don't wanna waste the whole day!

I wanna get in and get out!

Get Ron out the way.

I heard about my boy's store.

I'm trying to get this guy as the primary on the home
equity.

I wanna get him up front so they don't give us no
static.

All right.

Then we can go and talk.

and again.

Hey, baby!

I'm on my way to my new office in Jersey City!

I have something you might be interested in!
I'm on my way to Journal Square, to my new office!
How far out are you?
I'll be in Journal Square inside an hour.
OK.
So, I'll see you later.
We'll talk.

--------------------

MaBSOu:   Yeah. So, you wanna go with it?
          If it's less expensive, then you're OK?
          Yeah.
          Mm-hmm.
          Oh.
          Well, is it ugly?
          OK.
          All right.
          Oh.
          Right.
          All right.
          Yeah.
          What time is the meeting tomorrow?
          Right.
          OK.
          Well, good.
          Good.
          OK.
          No.
          What I thought what we could do is communicate
              with him.
          That's what I'd like to do.

Good.

All right.

Right.

All right.

Yeah.

Yeah.

Yeah.

Right.

Right.

Yeah.

No, there is no carport.

There's no other way because we have no garage.

I have to find out what the other bids are.

He paused as the conductor made an announcement.

What do you need and I'll do it.

And since Brian picked him out I'm sure he's good.

So, it's moving along.

So, call him tomorrow.

It's so hard to get a hold of him, I thought.

He's suffering.

He's dying.

He wants to get out.

Oh, the locksmith.

He's going to come tomorrow.

From who?

Well, OK.

Well, the train gets in at a quarter-of-ten and I'll get the
    stuff to him. It definitely won't take long.

OK, I'll see you.

He dialed again...

> Hello, Mike!
> How are things, my friend?
> Well, I won't be in New York Wednesday.
> But I will be on Thursday and Friday.
> We lost our main investor, so I'm still looking.
> I'm looking for something smaller.
> I have a few investors in New Jersey so I'm in the same
> position, trying to get money.
> I was going to come to New York on Friday with one of my
> investors. Do you wanna get together?
> Are you OK?
> Are you mad at me?
> (laughs)
> OK, so I'm definitely in on Friday, so we can get together
> then.
> OK, my friend.
> Ciao.
> Ciao.

and again.

> Hey.
> How are you, my friend?
> It's coming along.
> I lost an investor but I think I've got someone else.
> This guy bought licensing rights from Mattel and he's going
> to start a Barbie restaurant.
> You know, Barbie? The doll?
> Yeah.
> Brian was not very complimentary about it.

Well, he was like, "OK, we'll do the fucking Barbie thing!
But can we get **this** out of the way first?"
Yeah.
He wanted to get what he thought was more important
    going.
Yeah!
It's a great idea!
So, how are things going with you?
Oh yeah?
Yeah.
OK
I'll talk to you, my friend.

--------------------

MaBS1n:    Hey, Jerry!
           Good!
           Yeah.
           Yeah.
           Yeah.
           Right.
           Right.
           I don't think we could do it today.
           Not a publicity person.
           So the most productive thing is tell the publicity
               people who your V.P. is going with.
           Put together a wish list.
           Yeah.
           What?
           I'm sorry; we just went through a tunnel.
           Yeah, so put together a wish list and we can—
           Hello?

Hello?

Moments later...

Hey it's me.
Hey, sorry about that.
I'm just getting into Hoboken.
Yeah.
Put together a wish list for the publicity people.
I'll talk to Harry to see what we can do with the spots.
Great.
Great.
I'll talk to Harry and get back to you.

--------------------

MaBS9y:   Hi, John. It's Allen from Newmark & McLeod!
          I just thought I'd touch base.
          Yeah. I'm on the train to New York right now.
          Oh great!
          They never got back to you?
          I apologize for that.
          I didn't know.
          Great.
          Great.
          We're willing to accept liability for our contractors.
              But we're not willing to accept liability for the
              other contractors.
          We're not willing to accept liability for what the other
              contractors, employees, agents do or not do.
          If it is determined that we are 40% at fault—
          We're not trying to minimize our liability!

We just don't think it's fair for us to accept liability!

It's how much risk we are willing to accept or if the
third party is at fault!

I understand.

It's inconsequential.

Correct.

That'll be fine.

That'll be great.

I think it was part of the inventory.

Sure.

Sure.

That's fine.

OK.

That's fine.

While we're here I'll call Ted and tell him that everything is
OK and he can sign it right away.

OK.

(dials)

Hi, Ted. I'm in a conference call with Craig.

He's in agreement.

He's going to make the changes.

I suggest you print the copies immediately and send them
off and you're in business, buddy!

Congratulations, Craig!

--------------------

MaBS6q:   No kidding!
          No kidding!
          No kidding!
          No kidding!
          No kidding!

No kidding!

That would **not** be possible.

Yeah.

Number one, that would not be acceptable.

Yes.

Mm-hmm.

That is true. The problem is it needs to be set up in such a way that the contract is legal and binding.

And that any breach of the contract would be resolved in a um...a um...economical way.

No.

I'm not saying that you can't do **that**!

Mm-hmm.

Mm-hmm.

Mm-hmm.

Mm-hmm.

No, because if you state the fact that for the company— what is the name of the company?

OK.

Right.

Right.

Possibly.

Possibly.

Yeah.

Yeah.

Yes.

Yes.

That is very possible.

She is not working on this.

No.

No.

Mm-hmm.

Mm-hmm.

Hmm?

Mm-hmm.

Mm-hmm.

Uh-huh.

Indeed.

Yes.

That is not it.

Mm-hmm.

Mm-hmm.

Mm-hmm.

Mm-hmm.

That is true because you see that the hardware is not
    compatible.

And that is not the case.

No.

Call the payment to him and—

Yeah.

Mm-hmm.

Mm-hmm.

I'll be at the shop.

What?

That makes sense.

Abir?

You're breaking up.

What?

He looked at his phone and sighed heavily.

# EarBud

Wearing electronic earring-like tethers, the ubiquitous Earbud shares its music with all passengers around it, whether we want to hear it or not.

Deeply engrossed in getting its groove on, the Earbud will sometimes hum or sing quite loudly, completely unaware of its ill-delivered fits of key and vibrato. Even if it possesses an adequate singing voice, most of its fellow passengers don't care for the impromptu performance they are forced to endure.

I must admit that when one boards the train, I am curious about its taste in music. Ever sit next to one scrolling through its music library on its phone? Ever try to sneak a peek?

Sometimes when I hear music leaking through the Earbud's appendages, I am more concerned about the creature's hearing than annoyed with its lack of manners. Frankly, I don't blame it for playing its music so loudly. With the train populated by so many cellophiles and other loud-talking creatures, the need to shut them all out becomes urgent. Because of this, the Earbud presents a valid case for a pardon.

Instead of getting angry, I usually play "Name That Tune" by listening to the treble-laden sounds that leak from their buds. Try it. It's a real challenge because the only clues you'll have are the beats and the high notes from musical instruments. You might get lucky enough to hear some lyrics. With careful attention, you might be able to discern the difference between R&B and Rock songs. Hip Hop is very easy. Soon you'll find yourself so absorbed in the game, you may not even notice the cellophile just a few seats away.

Remember those walkie-talkie cell phones? I was fortunate enough to observe a cellophile using one, so it was an unexpected treat when I was able to hear **both** sides of a conversation!


FaCM8r:   You can get me but I can't get you!
REPLY:    Start answering the damned phone!
FaCM8r:   (laughs)
          I'm on my way to the office. I was going to go back but
          it's raining, so I'm not going.
REPLY:    Who's home?
FaCM8r:   Sharon and Marge are home.
REPLY:    OK.


--------------------


I joined this one already in progress:


REPLY:    I'm sorry. I'm so sorry.
MaCM7p:   I scheduled a meeting for 11:00?
REPLY:    You, Randy, Brad and Cindy.
MaCM7p:   All right. So I should be there at 11:00?
REPLY:    Thank you very much.
MaCM7p:   What?
REPLY:    I said, "Thank you very much." Enjoy the rest of your
          daaaayyyy!
MaCM7p:   Yeah. Sorry about that. I don't think this is working. I
          wanted to know about some of the changes on my
          idea.

CONDUCTOR:   Orange Station next. Ladies and gentlemen, I'd

like to remind you that cell phones and portable radios should be kept at minimum level. As hard as it is to believe, this **is** public transportation and there are other passengers on the train.

Amen, Mr. Conductor. Amen.

A male cellophile dialed a number and waited a few moments.

PHONE:   Please enter your personalized pass code.

He entered another set of numbers, then...

PHONE:   At the tone, begin recording your personal greeting.

An incoming call interrupted. He answered. This was funny because he must have owned one of those walkie-talkie phones. We could not hear the cellophile but we were able to hear the person on the other end!

VOICE:   Where are you?
         Could I come down and meet you?

PASSENGER:   Could you turn down your speakerphone?

VOICE:   No! No! No!
         Where the hell are you?

The passenger got up and approached the cellophile.

PASSENGER:   Excuse me. Could you turn off your speakerphone?

VOICE:   Are you at Highland Avenue now?

The passenger went back to her seat. Moments later, the cellophile was approached by a conductor.

CONDUCTOR:   Could you lower that? You gotta lower that.
             Thanks

PASSENGER:    I asked him twice.

From this point, we were able to hear the cellophile instead of the person on the other end.

MalE3d:    I don't wanna get in trouble.
           So, how about it?
           Yup!
           (laughs)
           Next stop is mine.
           I said next stop is mine!
           Forget about it.
           Forget about it!
           Forget about it!
           That's irrelevant!
           Everybody's saying that!
           Hello?
           Hello?
           Hello?

Be Considerate. Speak Softly

-- NJ Transit display

CalE5u:   Hi.
         I'm on the train at Penn station.
         I just thought I'd share my city news with you.
         I'm sorry to call you but I thought I'd share my city
             news with you.
         Just thought you might appreciate it.
         Some nonsense.
         I went upstairs to have a cigarette.
         And I had an allusion.
         I'm on the train.
         I'm on the 9:30.
         I should be out of the station at 9:30...10:30...11:30.
         I'll be at the station in maybe an hour.
         I was outside and there were all these people.
         My life is very sheltered.
         I've never seen this before.
         The train is packed.
         The train is four cars long and it's packed!
         What are all these people doing in New York at night?
         There's a guy walking around the track.
         What's up with that?
         There is nothing out there on the tracks to look at.
         What could there possibly be to look at?
         On the tracks?
         With a flashlight.
         But it's pretty.
         I've never seen anything like this.
         I just thought I'd share my city news with you.
         I though you might appreciate it.
         Oh! Guess what?
         That guy left all his presents in my room!
         In the guest room.

I looked and there were all these bags with jewelry in
   them!
(laughs)
And I'm asking, "What are we going to do with all these
   bags?"
And he said, "I'll take care of it."
We were all at the meeting and he left all these bags and
   they all had watches in them!
I'm like, "What am I going to do with all these bags?"
And every one had a watch in them!
Are you guys in bed?
Well, I'm going to be entering a tunnel, so I might lose you.
We have a little time
OK.
Bye.

--------------------

FaMS6q:   Right.
          Right.
          Yeah.
          That's what I'd do.
          Right.
          OK.
          That's what I'll do.
          Right.
          Right.
          Right.
          Right.
          He was still thinking he could do the plans on
          Wednesday.
          I'm going into a tunnel, so if I lose you, I'll call you
             back.

What I was thinking about on Friday is to gather all my
    notes.

I've been writing.

Yes.

Yes.

I can do that.

I can cancel four people and pay for dinner.

I'm losing you.

Kathy?

Kathy?


Once we got out of the tunnel, she dialed again.


Hi there.

Where'd we leave off?

OK.

Yeah. We should.

Titles are two different things. So whatever it is, it would
    be good because me and titles are—

This would be a helpful conversation for me.

OK, let's do two things—

Uh-huh.

OK. That I will do tomorrow.

Let me see how it goes on Friday and I'll see you on
    Saturday.

OK. Bye.


She dialed again.


Hi, Jane. I had to call my curator.

He needs this and he needs titles. And it's all this stuff.

My stress level just shot up.

Getting this done.

They're going to have money.

And she's just anxious.

I try to act like it's all together with her and—

Right.

And you know she talks about the politics of this.

And you know I had to get her off the phone.

Yeah.

I'll talk to you.

Bye.

--------------------

FaMS1j:   So, you can start tomorrow?

OK.

OK.

I know.

There will be some changes.

OK but just so you know, I am going to make some changes.

Just so you know, OK?

I know it's almost done but there will be some changes.

It is.

It is.

I know.

Eddie has it at 90% but there are some things that need to change.

OK.

OK.

OK.

OK.

OK.

She hung up and dialed.

Hi.

I need you to do me a favor.

I need you to look at the layout and see if there are items
that need to change.

Like, the flow of it.

Item by item.

Well I-

I think it would be better if you do it than it would for me
to do it.

It would be more consistent.

Like, the category headings and stuff like that.

Eddie-

Eddie-

Eddie-

If we can't do it today, I'll do it!

Yeah!

I'll do it because I want it to go out tomorrow!

I need it to go out tomorrow!

So, I'll do it because I don't want to work on it over the
weekend!

But I'll do it tomorrow!

If we can't do it today.

It's not a big deal!

Bye!

--------------------

MaEX7f:  Hello?
          Yes. I was there a half hour ago and I left my college
             ring.
          Hello?
          Hello?

He closed his eyes and pressed his face against the window.
Moments later he dialed again.

   Hello?
   Yeah I just called about the ring.
   Sorry. I'm on the train and I lost the signal.
   No, I can't. I'm on my way home.
   I can be there at 6:00 or 6:30.
   That would be very nice of you. Thank you very much.


                    --------------------


MaCM3r:  Hi, Mom. It's Lenny. I'm on the 6:47 train. Call me on
             my cell. xxx-xxxx.
          OK?
          Bye.

He dialed another number...

   Hi, it's Lenny. I'm on the 6:47 train. Call me on my cell. xxx-
      xxxx. OK?
   Bye.

and another.

Hi, Mom It's Lenny. I'm on the 6:47 train. Give me a call on
my cell. xxx-xxxx.
OK? Bye.

--------------------

MaCM4f:   Hello?

This is Tom Willis.

I was wondering. Can washers and dryers be placed in
the apartments upstairs?

No? That's what I figured.

The building won't allow it.

I guess it sounds silly with the laundry room to have
them upstairs.

No, he wasn't able to sell it because he had to wait
for the deal to be over.

OK. I'll talk to you later.

Bye.

--------------------

FaCM5w:   Hi.

I'm on the train to New York.

Any messages?

Fax?

Can you read them to me?

(long pause)

Here's what I want you to do. Take out the packet.

That is so inappropriate for you.

Resolve that thing!

OK, what else do you have?

No, don't do anything with that!

Yeah.

What is it?

Yeah.

Yeah, why don't you do that?

I'll be there in half an hour. Then you can work on some
 other stuff.

OK.

I'll talk to you later. My cell phone is going out.

--------------------

MalE7j:   Two reeds.

Two broken.

How do I find out about getting more?

That would be awesome!

That's perfect.

Yeah.

Oh yeah, OK.

OK.

Yeah.

Beautiful.

It's probably cheaper to get the moiré than the other
 ones.

Yeah.

They're expensive!

Everything's expensive!

How you doin'?

I just got on the train to go back to Jersey.

Yeah.

I couldn't believe it.

Half the class didn't show up.

I'm like, damn. You're only in Jersey and you couldn't make
   it?
Say that again?
Wow, that's great!
Psychology for kids?
Yeah.
Yeah.
The only thing I could say in their defense is when I was in
   college, they gave us so much work.
Right.
Yeah.
Right.
I know when I was in college I was bogged down.
Yeah.
Yeah.
Uh-huh.
No.
Yeah.
Yeah.
Yeah.
(laughs)
Yeah.
Well, it's not so bad, I guess.
Say again?
Yeah.
That's great.
I ran into so many out of college who were into it.
Who could play faster?
Really?
First, I heard he was an alto player.
First, I heard he was an alto player.
Wow!

Great!
Right.
And he disappeared.
Yeah.
Yeah.
Oh, that's great!
(laughs)
That's funny!
I don't know her but I think I met her once.
I think they went to California.
Alto Acres.
Wow!
(laughs)
Yeah!
Yeah!
Yeah!
Oh boy!
Oh my!
Oh yeah!
(laughs)
Really?
Right.
Really?
Yeah!
Wow!
(laughs)
That's what you said?
With Lex?
I loved that!
(laughs loudly)
See, I saw all that stuff at Costco!
I saw all that stuff at Costco!

And I had some wine stains on my carpet and I got a
couple of bottles and got it up.
So, maybe I'll get you some.
Oh, she's lost it!
She's lost it!
Yep!
Life is short.
I think I saw a friend of mine.
Oh.
Oooh my God!
(laughs)
Aaaawww!
Right.
Right.
Right.
Well, I'm so glad I called.
Send me an email.
I really appreciate you getting them.
Yeah.
Better than many.
Yeah.
Yeah.
Yeah.
Yep.
I could just look at them.
Ooooh!
Yeah!
All right.
Yeah.
Yeah.
Yeah, great talking to you, Tom!

# Text, Don't Talk

For those of you who are new to riding the train, the first and last open cars are designated Quiet Commute Cars. This means no cellular phone use is permitted in said cars.

If you must talk with your travel companion, it is preferable that you move to another car. But if you keep your voices low, you may stay in the Quiet Car.

Also, ring tones and notifications should be turned off. And if you are among the uneducated that still leave their key tones on, those should be silenced as well.

Conductors, please make a better effort to enforce the Quiet Commute Car rules. Make sure that the Quiet Commute signs are displayed in hard-to-miss locations in all Quiet Cars. Set up the automated announcements to remind people of the Program. And please remember, some people are rebellious and/or not so smart and need to be made to behave, so don't be afraid to admonish those individuals.

But, if these words happen to fall on deaf ears, I submit the following appeal...

# Jam On It! (a message for the FCC)

One day, I heard a news report about a black-market device, which was being used in the fight against cellophiles. It's called the "jammer". It interferes with the cell phone's ability to make or receive calls. Much to my chagrin, it has been deemed illegal.

Ladies and gentlemen of the FCC, please reconsider your position concerning jammers.

Imagine the valuable service this product could provide the public. Of course, preventive measures would have to be made to ensure that no one could use it for untoward endeavors. Also, there must be a means of deactivating the device in the event of an actual emergency. I'm sure that you could conjure up a gadget that could satisfy everyone's needs.

This is the Quiet Car! If you can't do it, don't choose it!

-- Conductor upon arrival at the station

MaCM9l:   Hi.

I had a number for him that I picked up and I seem to
have lost it.

I was calling to see if I could get it from you.

(long pause)

No, I understand.

Well, maybe you could give me his office number.

(another long pause)

Yeah I know but it's the only number I had.

OK.

No, no problem.

Bye.

--------------------

FaCM3z:   Hey!

Good! How are you?

What happened?

Hold on one second.

OK. What's your number?

OK.

OK.

OK.

OK.

She dialed.

Hey.

Why is this better?

Why?

Hmm.

Meaningless?

Meaningless after a while.

Mundane?

(laughs)

That's when you go crazy!

That's Larry Huber.

So, where do you think you wanna go?

Well, think about it this way; you'll have a year and a half left.

Come to school with me.

Oh.

I don't know what to tell you.

That's frustrating.

Yeah.

It's just boring.

It's like, think of something new.

No, I don't.

(laughs)

Well, there are no—

Like, we all go other places and we all look, but there's no way to find them.

You should come work this summer.

So much fun!

There's no more Ryan, Britt or Den.

Or Paulina.

It's really good times!

No.

All you have to do is call.

You know what Clara did?

She called two weeks before camp and she got a job!

Oh my God!

I just saw the best thing ever!

I'm so excited!

Oh my God!

Oh my God!

Oh my God!

Oh my God!

I might pee myself!

One thing you have to do...

See my dad.

Yeah.

Don't worry! Just see him.

And see my family.

See my family or they are going to kick your ass!

(laughs loudly)

Oh my God!

Everyone's going to be so shocked!

But you have to tell them that you want it to be a surprise.

Guess who's going to be there?

Andre Ford!

They'll put out a list and they'll put his name on!

(laughs)

He'll be like, "What the fuck?"

They'll be like, "Oh my God!"

There's another Glenn Fallon!

Oh my God—

You mean your application?

You're going to love Barry!

He is like, the chillest man alive!

What's the name of that boy?

The one who was so crazy?

He was the best camper ever!

(laughs)

Secret.

Cooler than Jerry.

No, cooler than Sally!

He—

Yeah!

Yeah!

He's like, the coolest guy alive!

Or so he thinks so!

He wants to be a rock star!


This was my stop.


--------------------


FaCM4x:   9:11.

Yeah.

I got a Chinese calendar.

Oh my God!

Well, you shouldn't be sick for another year!

Yeah.

Yeah.

Yeah.

Yeah.

Yeah.

Yeah.

Yeah.

Yeah.

I don't know.

I saw it but I didn't have time to bring up the links.

Did it have pictures?

No.

She said I should bring the dog home.

She said I could bring you home since you're the year of the dog.

(laughs)

You're the year of the dog!

Mine was the rat!

What's hers?

1/54?

Yeah she's 1/54.

OK.

I'll see you at 9:11.

--------------------

FaCM2c:   Daniel san!

How are things going at the studio?

How are you?

Yeah.

I saw Mom and Dad in Phoenix.

They had a bad trip over.

She had a bad time on the plane and she'll never fly
ever again.

I have the files for you.

I have it on disk.

It's on a Quicken file but you might be able to use it as
a TIFF file.

OK?

All right.

Well, let me know what happens.

Ciao.

Bye.

--------------------

MalE6j:   Hello?

Hello?

Yeah, nine.

I'm on the train.

I'll come back early.

What's that?

Hello?

Hello?

Hello?

--------------------

FalEOd:   Hi!

No. I'm still here.

I'll call you when we're a little bit out.

I'll call you when I get out of the tunnel thing.

OK.

Bye.

About ten minutes later she dialed.

Yeah.

We haven't left yet.

Do you know I'm so hungry now?

I'm hungry.

I haven't eaten yet!

I'm so hungry!

There was a problem with some train and it affected some other train. And I like, stayed late at work to be nice.

I stayed to be nice and now I'm like, "Damn that!"

OK.

Bye.

She dialed again...

Hi, Mike. It's Laura. Just calling to see if you need me. I'll
call you later. Bye.

and again...

Hi!
When are you going back to school?
When do you have class?
I have to work from 11:00 to 10:00.
I thought you might be in the city today.
You might have to come towards me because I have
limited time.
So, is that OK?
I'll get some time during my dinner break and go.
By the way, thanks you guys for coming to visit me.
That was real nice of you.
Call me on my cell and we'll do it then.
OK.
Bye.

and again...

What time is it?
It's like, supposed to be like, a forty-minute ride from like,
Penn Station.
OK.
I'll call you later.

and again...

Where are you right now?
I'm on the 8:02 that was delayed.

I'll call you when I get to South Orange.

OK.

Bye.

---------------------

OK, maybe some of these calls were important, but the cellophiles should have kept their voices down!

FaEX1z:   Hi.

I'm on the 8:44 train.

I have no idea.

It's a local.

You know?

It's the 8:44.

No. It hasn't moved yet.

I'm in Hoboken.

I'm not in the city.

Probably because of the derailment.

Twenty is probably more fair than fifteen.

I'll call you when I get near.

OK.

---------------------

FaEX8p:   Hi.

How are you?

I'm on the train.

I'll get in at 9:28

OK.

I'll see you later.

Bye.

----------------------

MaEX5v:   Hi
I'm on the train.
The New York Direct broke down and the train at
Mountain Station was packed.
Hello?
Hello?
Hello?
Hello?

----------------------

MaEX1s:   Hi, it's Sam.
I'm on the Hoboken train.
My train broke down in Summit.
I think I'll be there within an hour, I don't know.
I have to take the PATH or the ferry, so I'll see you
    when I get there.

----------------------

MaEX9i:   Hey, Harry. It's Andy.
My train broke down, so I'm going to be delayed.

----------------------

FaEX4l:   Hi, honey. It's me. I might be able to go. I'm on the
    train. It's 9:50.
Nothing happened, but I'll tell you all about it later. I'll

try you on your cell, OK? It's 9:53, so when you hear this, you need to call. It's 9:53, so when you hear this, you need to call.

She dialed another number.

Hi, Penelope, It's me. It's 9:55. I'm on the train to the city. I don't know if you're in town today but give me a call. My number is xxx-xxxx.

---------------------

The following conversation took place the day after a major blackout hit New York and other parts of the northeast:

FaOA4u:   Do you understand what I'm saying?

I spent all day to get here! It took me so long to get to this station!

I don't have any money!

You know, you haven't said one nice thing to me since I called you!

What do you mean? I was in the city!

Where else was I going to be?

I was with my friends!

I wasn't by myself!

So you'd rather I try to come home alone? In the dark?

Worried about what?

Why would you worry?

I'm trying to understand where you're coming from! I was in the city, in a crisis!

There was no way to get home!

I was with Diane and Maria!

I have no money!

I wasn't going to coming home by myself!

Why would you worry if you knew I was safe with friends?

Oh, so you think I was with some guy and not my friends?

Well, I have to say, I'm disappointed in you!

You didn't handle yourself well at all!

I'm very disappointed in you!

Because I thought you would have been a little stronger
     than the way you're portraying yourself now!
Do you know I have two cents to my name right now?
That's why I'm mad at you!
Yes! That's why I'm mad at you!
So, you're at the country club?
No. What time are you getting off?
Why do you want to know?
I'm trying to! That's why I'm asking you when you're
     getting off work!
I told you I stayed at Diane's!
No!
It was dark so we just sat there!

She hung up.

--------------------

FaCM4l:   Hey!
          Hey!
          I was calling you guys before I left!
          OK.
          I'll get there around 7:30.
          I could get off at South Orange, too.
          I could get off at South Orange, too.
          All right.
          I'll call you guys later.
                    --------------------

MaOA2q:   I'm in the Penn Station waiting area.
          I finished my sorting.

I finished my sorting.

I'm scheduled to leave on the 9:35. It should get there around 11:00 or something.

So, can you pick me up?

You're gonna have to because I don't have anything else.

I'm sitting in the seating area.

How can I miss the train?

I can give you the number of the train if I can read this thing!

I can't find the number on this thing!

Well, just be there around 11:00!

--------------------

MaCM9e:   I'm at the station.

(laughs)

Me too!

You know, Jay, let me play it for you!

You know—

OK!

You know I'd like it!

I'm in for it.

And if you need anything—

I'm in Newark!

No.

No.

(looks around)

These are pretty pleasant people.

(looks around again)

OK.

Here's my train.

OK.

---------------------

MaOA3y:    Yo.

What's up?

I just got on the train to Dover.

I went out for some drinks.

I didn't have my phone on. That's why I didn't get
your call.

Yeah.

Yeah.

Yeah.

So, I'm all bad.

(laughs)

I think I met that kid—

Hello?

Hello?

(slams the phone on his lap)

Damn!

---------------------

MaOA9r:    I'm on the train.

I'm on the train.

I'll be there at 9:40...9:20.

Is that too late for you?

(angrily) Have a good night!

---------------------

FalE0q:   Hello?

Hi.

I'm on my way home.

Why?

What's wrong?

I'm really like, three hours away.

What?

Do you wanna talk?

OK.

You're welcome.

OK.

Bye.

--------------------

MaHR8e:   There was a guy named Chang and he was on top of
everything!

There's got to be something going on in Texas
because my backup was Ned Tubman.

I'll cut him a check on the back end!

Oooooooh!

That's even better!

You supposed to call me when you get something
like that so I could get a cut!

If you got some TLS and ELC!

Mm-hmm!

Charmin is fine!

Feels just as good!

You set me up with that man!

And I'm climbing poles and climbing rafters!

Had to lock up the liquor cabinet and everything!

Who brought the Thunderbird?
I deliberately signed up for training because I
   wanted to get paid for training!
I told him nobody's walking out!
Because school starting soon!
College tuition and clothes!
Ain't nobody walking out!
The fall line is about to come out and I need some shoes!
The only thing I got out of it is if the wires go out, I can go
   out there and fix it!
I laughed because you haven't talked to this girl!
What paperwork gives you an address?
The LD was bad.
I had to tell him, "You are getting in the way of me bringing
   in some revenue!
How far do I have to send this e-mail?
I'm already in the doghouse!
They said they gonna dock me!
I'm gonna wind up eating at the Chicken Shack!
(laughs)
He's too busy being a pretty boy.
He's a pretty boy.
It's at the point where John's talking about selling stuff.
If I lose you, it's because I'm in a tunnel.
Are you there?

He dropped the phone, picked it up and continued.

No.
The train is in the tunnel.
When I was in Brazil he was trying to get something going
And I know what he was doing.

But when Trytek called me about what they needed, don't
   you know I read what I needed to know?

He need to go somewhere.

Put him in a basket and send him to hell!

Forty years.

Mm-hmm.

He been there forty years, girl!

He need to retire.

Mm-hmm!

Ooooh!

God no!

We'll open up a chicken & rib shack in East Orange!

He never bothered anybody.

But when he needed a TSS line he never came to me.

I'm mad at Basil!

I'ma grind that bitch down to sage!

I'll put that spice in a grinder!

Barry told Chelsea she didn't know how much paperwork
   they did!

And you ain't talk to her?

Mm-hmm!

Mm-hmm!

And here's the gotcha. The gotcha is over the customers
   use ISPs from multiple vendors!

Mm-hmm!

You'll see when you look it up.

I was on the phone till 9am!

I was on with Stewart and I thought I might as well do it
   myself!

Dave said he looks good in a suit and that's about it!

When he becomes vice president he'll have to remember
   that.

But there was no reason to hold the contract!

That's what I'm tellin' you!

It was signed when I got there!

No!

Which one?

That's a new one 'cause you gotta back-door that one!

So maybe he don't have no power but he know that
    legalese!

No!

No!

GNI networks from Manhattan to Berkley Heights.

So I had to tell him the deal!

Mm-hmm!

Mm-hmm!

You need to understand my company is worth five billion!

Mm-hmm!

Yours ain't nothin'!

The only brother in the bar was me!

They all fightin' and stuff!

You don't want your boss to ever call me after I've been
    out with Mike!

It's 9:05. What are you still doing there?

I'm gonna tell Pattie!

(laughs)

I gotta tell Big Momma!

Mm-hmm!

I heard about that, girl!

Now I know why Mike wanted me to come in!

He wanted me to serve his ass!

I gotta whisper this.

I forgot Mike is a girl.

Remember when he said the dog's name was Mike?

But it's a girl dog?

My friend had to put pads on his dog.

Mm-hmm.

You should have told him, "I didn't want the dog! You do it!"

What did they do before?

So, the dog don't like pads?

(laughs)

She won't come down 'cause she's embarrassed!

(laughs louder)

She don't like the pads!


He got off at East Orange.

Have you ever tried, in a discreet manner, to make someone aware that his zipper is undone? How about the fact that he has food on his teeth? Did he get the message? If not, this is what it's like trying to make a cellophile aware of its behavior.

A comical series of events take place when a cellophile is broadcasting a call. Previously concealed heads rise slowly from behind the seats, (usually wearing a frown) scanning the area to determine the source of the commotion.

Moments later, you will hear people clearing their throats, accompanied by coughing and sneezing. Heavy sighs are heaved from behind the sound of newspaper and magazine pages being snapped. Alas, these sophisticated attempts to get the cellophile's attention will never enter the first ear, let alone go out the other.

Please keep those innocent passengers in your thoughts and prayers.

FalO5d:   Hello?

How are you?

I'm on the train.

I know.

A little later.

Dana wanted to come over and play.

And I thought I could finally get to meet this woman.

And I thought he could have someone to play with and
then I completely forgot and I thought 'Oh no! He's
not going to have a playmate!'

The people are very friendly.

It has a southwestern feel to it.

Very friendly, without all the attitude.

My mother is coming over and—

Hello?

Hello?

Hi.

I lost you.

(laughs)

OK.

I'll talk to you later.

OK.

Bye.

--------------------

MaBS9f:   Linda?

It's Pete.

How are you?

Do you know how much it cost for San Diego for eight
hours?

I talked to somebody and the number they gave me

was kinda high.

I asked for a price in San Diego for an eight-hour shift and they gave me a figure of $1500 an hour. I think that's way too much money.

Someone in their finance department.

Mexico and Toronto at $1000 per hour.

That's for hydration.

I'll forward you a copy.

Yeah.

OK.

Very good.

Thank you very much.

He dialed again.

Yeah, Alice?

What happened with that guy, Gerard?

Did he call back?

Did you ask him how long it would take?

Because I'd like to secure that line of credit Friday.

It's gonna take that long?

Ask him why it can't be done sooner.

Because I wanna get this done!

OK?

Yeah, definitely call him because I wanna call him.

OK.

--------------------

FaCM3e:    You gonna pick me up from Boston?

No?

Why are you laughing?

No!

Tell me!

Are you with her already?

Why are you out in this weather?

Are you in a truck?

Whatever.

I'm not telling you!

(laughs)

All right.

Where are you going?

Elizabeth?

Yeah.

All right.

Bye.


--------------------


FaSB4q:   Hi.

I'm on the train.

I definitely shouldn't have went out.

I know it wasn't smart but they asked me and I said I would.

I know it wasn't smart but they asked me and I said I would.

We went to some place called "Under the Tunnel."

It's just a bar.

I didn't even eat lunch.

I forgot my lunch.

I'm starving.

What?

I can't hear you.
The train is packed.
Hello?
Hello?

She dialed again.

Hello?
How you doin'?
What are you doing?
I went out for drinks.
I know, but they asked me to.
Are you at a bar?
I can't believe you're at a bar right now!
OK.
Bye.

--------------------

MalE7c:   Yeah.
          The usual one was waiting for me.
          Yeah.
          Yeah.
          Yeah.
          I haven't listened to him yet.
          OK.
          All right.
          OK.
          Yeah.
          Bye.

--------------------

FalE0x:  Hi, it's me.
         I'm looking at an article about the Bruce Springsteen
            concert.
         It says it sold out in fourteen minutes.

A conductor made an announcement.

         So, I'll talk to you later, OK?
         All right.
         Bye-bye.


                    --------------------


MaCM8h:  Hey! You there?
         I hope so! Well, I'll see you.


                    --------------------


MaCM2k:  Hello?
         Jay?
         It's Bob.
         Did you receive the program?
         Good.
         Ok.
         I'll see you later.
         Bye.

The greatest benefit I enjoyed while writing this book is the fact that my subjects had no idea they were being observed, very much unlike the subjects on "reality" shows on TV.

When people know they are being watched, reality goes out the window and is replaced by a "make love to the camera" performance. Shrink or shine. Some people will even invent a character to spice up the show. If there were any drama kings or queens on my journey, these folks were keeping it real.

FaCM7g:  I pretty much hate every aspect of life.
Sometimes it's just hard to get out of this kind of
    funk.
You know, I'd rather hear you talk than talk about it.
Well, it's not your mess and-

(conductor made an announcement)
    ...he's crazy.
McDonald's characters.
I love my costume!
Yeah.
I'm going to be the Hamburglar!
Striped shirt, cape, hat, striped pants and a mask.
What are you wearing?
Not like last year!
Yeah, like, "What's that crap?"
It's like, "Hi, you suck!"
(laughs)
We're so gonna win this year!
My boss is going to be Mayor McCheese and everyone
    else has the option to be a fat kid and shit like that!
Because of the whole McDonald's thing!
Maybe we should get some burger wrappers!
We are **so** winning!
I wanted everyone to go as the Hamburglar!
Yeah.
One is great but five is hilarious!
That would be funny to see five Hamburglars walking
    around!
(laughs)
We only travel in packs!
(laughs loudly)

I also thought about going as Grimace!
(laughs)
Could you imagine five Grimaces walking by?
People would be tripping up!
(laughs even louder)
That's what I wanted to do but nobody wanted to do it and
I was like, "Fuck that!"
I'm going to lose you.
I'm going into a tunnel.

--------------------

FalO9k:   Hello?

Thank you! You're so sweet!
I just got on the train!
You're so sweet!
You're so sweet!
You're so sweet!
You're such a good friend!
What are you doing tomorrow?
Are there any bars open?
That's so cool!
That's so nice!
Very nice!
Oh wow!

A conductor approached and asks her to tone it down.

That sound like a fun weekend!
OK. Bye!

--------------------

FalE1b:     64% of the audience thought it was great.
            My daughter's success would play into the Kingdom
                whether she knows it or not.
            She's planning a trip to Greece to visit her spiritual dad.

A man sitting behind her furrowed his brow and stared at the
seat in front of him, mustering all his Jedi skills to will FACH1b to
shut up. When she started reciting Scripture, he leaned back,
stared at the ceiling, heaved a heavy sigh and said, 'Fuck me!'

It all seemed to go downhill from there.

At this time, a male cellophile entered the scene. He was one of
those brothas who was in his mid thirties but still dressed like he
was twelve. He walked the length of the car asking, 'You still get
the dial-up sound?' over and over.

Another cellophile was talking in that ghetto speak that makes
black folks who do not speak that way embarrassed that they
have to share a racial group with such vocabularily-challenged
individuals.

Moments later, a phone rang. FACH1b answered with an 'Amen'.
Her conversation was peppered with more religious affirmations.
She also offered some philosophy; 'We are like an oasis in the
wilderness...' kind of stuff.

Yet another cellophile made a call to announce that she's late for
an appointment and that she would be there shortly.

FACM1b's phone rang again. She offered more scripture, along with a string of 'Yea's (the biblical pronunciation) and a declaration of 'having on the Armor of The Lord' as we pulled into Penn Station.

--------------------

The following exchange took place on the South Orange station platform:

MaCM8d:   Hi.

          I heard.

          Well, Tim said that everyone was screaming at each other at the top of their lungs.

          He'd never seen anything like it before.

          Yeah.

          They were really yelling at each other.

A man approached the cellophile.

HERO:   Do you have to talk so loudly?

MaCM8d:   I don't know what you're talking about.

HERO:   Unfortunately, we know everything you're talking about. We can hear every word you're saying.

We never heard another word from MaCM8d.

--------------------

FaMS4h:   So we'll fix it, that's all!

          Well, they have three days.

          Jen isn't at fault here.

          And we have three days!

You have three days!
You have three days!
You see what I'm saying?
We have three days!
Call me when something important happens!
(laughs)
So, what else is happening?
That's not really all that important.
OK.
Bye.

--------------------

MaCM5i:    Do they even use currency in Columbia?
Have they actually moved on to using money?
So, you're working at that restaurant?
You need some dough?
Dude, I saw that movie "The Hangover". It was
    fuckin' awesome!
Let's go see it tonight!
I would love to see it with you, just to see your
    reaction!
I would be able to tell you the scenes!
I would enjoy watching you enjoy it!
Dude, it's Friday night!
Yeah, let's do something!
Yeah!
My phone might die, so I'll talk to you later.

He dialed again.

Aw, come on!
OK, but you gotta do it in **that** voice.

I'm good. How are you?

It's great to hear your voice.

Sometimes I like to call your voice mail just to hear your voice.

I could listen to you for hours.

I would marry you this second.

I just saw that movie "The Hangover". It was fuckin' awesome!

No. They're trying to find the groom.

Oh, I thought you asked if they were trying to find the bride.

No, they're trying to find the groom.

They wake up and he's gone and they trace backwards to find him.

I showed up at work in just a T-shirt and flip-flops, but my boss was there.

I just told him "I had no idea you were going to be here."

He was like "No big deal. I'm cutting your hours in half.

"Yeah, they love me.

You know why that is?

Because I'm so youthful.

I gotta go because I'm on the train.

Did you get the text with my address? OK. Make a right when you get to Northfield Avenue. Come down the hill. You're gonna pass Seton Hall Prep. Then, at the next big interception, make a right.

-- Cellophile giving directions to its nest

Ladies and Gentlemen, may I have your attention, please?

The next and last station stop is: Final Thoughts.

If you didn't place them on the seat next to you, please check the overhead luggage racks for all the lessons you learned on this trip. And place all inappropriate behavior in waste receptacles located on the station's platform. For your betterment, watch your manners after reading this book. If you have small children, please lead by example, using the counsel contained herein as a guide. If you need additional directions or information, please go back to page one and go over the instructions for information you might have missed the first time you read this book.

Thank you for riding with Commutication: A Look At Life On The Rails.

And please, grow up.

# Final Thoughts

Humans have made some amazing technological advances. Everything has been improved in ways never imagined fifteen, ten, even five years ago. Everything except themselves.

There is an old saying that says money does not breed class. It is also unfortunate how the worst human characteristics are amplified through the use of technology. We cannot blame the apparatus when cellophiles misuse their phones. The internet is not the culprit when people misbehave on social media platforms.

Dr. Martin Luther King, Jr. had a dream that one day a man will not be judged by the color of his skin, but by the content of his character. Well, I have seen the content of man's character and I am disappointed to say that humans have a long way to go before Dr. King's dream comes to pass.

I have witnessed the true nature in humans emerge when they thought no one was watching. I have seen the old woman making her way slowly down the stairs, while the young woman behind her glared at the woman in front of her, wishing she would just give up and die already, not once considering the fact that one day, she too will find herself in the older woman's position.

Allow me to illustrate another testimony concerning the evil of humans:

As the train makes its way to Hoboken or New York, the lights go out temporarily between Secaucus and the tunnel. During that time, I have seen white women grip their purses tighter because they happen to be sitting near black men.

Some might say that this is a "natural" reaction. This is a willfully ignorant statement. She has been trained to behave this way by parents, friends, the media or all three. The only way this "natural" reaction could possibly hold any weight is if the woman is in fact, a dog. An animal that is trained to attack a certain group of people does not possess the ability to judge a person on his/her merit. It will only do what it is trained to do. Real humans know right from wrong.

I developed an intense dislike for cellophiles and others after observing them for a few years, which is why I had to take a break halfway through my studies.

As much as I dislike cellophiles, I have no choice but to accept them, maybe even love them. Tolerance, no...pity has kept me from snatching a cellophile's phone and chucking it off the train at the next stop, to the delight of the other passengers.

After gathering all the data I needed for this book, I realized that cellophiles (and some humans) are no different from our own family members. They endear and enrage. We just have to appreciate them for all their feats and fails.
Cellophiles and humans must learn to ride the rails together. We must assume the roles of Unger and Madison, forced to share our trains without driving each other crazy. This task, rail riders, falls heavily upon the shoulders of the more highly evolved species of commuter.

I'll tell you why. Cellophiles are rude, self-centered and thoughtless. Their evolutionary process will probably span a decade or two before they develop the skills for text messaging. I am not making excuses for their inappropriate behavior. I am only suggesting that it is up to the more advanced beings to forgive their limited counterparts, the same way we would forgive a pet for soiling the carpet. For now, the cellophile can change its habits no easier than it would be for us to develop other means of delivering air to our lungs.

The cellophile's quest for fame, no matter how fleeting, is very personal. They want to remind us - and themselves - that people love them and enjoy having them around. They need to know that someone is thinking about them when they're not around. They take great comfort in the knowledge that their presence brings joy to someone else's life. They need to be a part of some connection that validates their existence.

Their hopes and dreams are no more valid than ours, but you don't hear **us** shouting our aspirations of worthiness for everyone to hear. **We** don't engage in narcissistic attempts to prove that we are valuable members of society. What makes **them** so special?

MaBSOu. A Barbie restaurant? Is this a joke? Was this idea was so groundbreaking that you could not wait to make this call in the privacy of your home or office? I had to listen to you go on and on about how this endeavor was going to make a killing. Well, guess what? A few years have passed and I haven't heard anything about this restaurant yet. Apparently I'm not the only one who thought it was a bad idea.

MaOA4k. Get over the fact that your ex girlfriend took everything that ever meant anything to you. Pull your pants up, wipe your nose and man up!

FaCM7x, if I wanted to learn how to make matzos lasagna, I would buy a cookbook.

Dressing up as the Hamburglar for Halloween? Are you serious, FaCM7g? McDonald's doesn't even use that character anymore!

FalO5u, I'll bet any amount of money that the person on the other end was not interested in your "city news". Train tracks and signals have to be maintained, that's why there were people walking around on them. They had flashlights because it was nighttime. Yes, your life is too sheltered. Get out more.

MaOA6a, if you don't want to give him money, don't give him money! In fact, throw the moocher out of your home if you're so tired of him!

FaCM6l, nobody cares that you go to Lana to get your hair done!

I hope your child is feeling better now, FalO1k, but we did not have to hear about her being sick. Listening to what she was going through was quite disturbing. It made the rest of us very uncomfortable. You really should have waited till you got home to make that call.

MaCM3x:     (reading its phone) Holy Shit!
            What the fuck?!
            They traded Odell Beckham?!

HERO 1:   Quiet Car!
HERO 2:   Quiet Car!

MaCM3x:   Sorry

You have chosen the Quiet Car! If that's not your M.O., get out!

-- Conductor upon entering the car

Again, this is the Quiet Car! If you can't handle it, don't sit here!

-- same Conductor before leaving the car

Now is a great time to show off your text messaging skills.


--AT&T billboard

# About the Author

Nygel 'Cheeky Monkey' Worthington was born in an undisclosed part of England. His father, William was a pharmacist and his mother Jenna, was a schoolteacher. Mysteriously, the date and time of his birth are unknown.

At a very young age, Nygel showed an insatiable interest in electronics. He was able to repair many devices, even modifying them to improve their performance. He became very popular among the locals, who referred to him as 'Gadget Inspector', a twist on the title of an American animated series. Soon, he began creating his own gadgets and caught the attention of several electronics companies around the world.

Despite his success, he grew weary of corporate culture and decided his skills could be better put to use serving The Royal Air Force. While the true nature of his assignments is still kept classified, he excelled in every challenge the military had to offer.

After an honorable discharge, it is believed he divided his time between unspecified military "consulting" work and playing bass guitar for various local rock and pop bands in Swindon, Liverpool and Sheffield. He was passed over for a spot in a band he thought 'had real potential'. While he refuses to disclose the name of the band, he said the chap who got the spot was an exceptional musician and a good songwriter to boot. The band went on to achieve cult-status success in the 1980s and 1990s,

Worhtington disappeared for several years after that unsuccessful audition, resurfacing in a location only describe as "Somewhere in New Jersey."

Made in the USA
Middletown, DE
13 May 2021